Matengo Folktales

recorded and translated by
Joseph L. Mbele
with commentaries

1999

Copyright © 1999 by Joseph L. Mbele

ISBN 0-7414-0028-6

Published by:

Infinity Publishing.com
519 West Lancaster Avenue
Haverford, PA 19041-1413
Info@buybooksontheweb.com
www.buybooksontheweb.com
Toll-free (877) BUY BOOK
Local Phone (610) 520-2500
Fax (610) 519-0261

Printed in the United States of America
Printed on Recycled Paper
Published February-2001

Contents

Preface

For more than a hundred years, people have collected and published African folktales and other folklore in various journals and books. Sometimes they have published these materials in the original language, with or without translations into a European language, and sometimes they have published only the translations. This work is continuing.

However, there are still many African societies whose tales have not been recorded and published. From some societies we have only a small selection of tales, or songs, or some other form of folklore. There is thus still much work to be done.

The tales in this collection come from the Matengo, who live in southern Tanzania, East Africa, on the eastern side of Lake Nyasa. They inhabit a mountainous region, between 5000 and 6000 feet above sea level. The land is cool for much of the year, and quite cold from April to July. The Matengo are hard working peasants; they grow coffee, maize, beans, peas, wheat, potatoes, pumpkins, cassava, and a few other crops, including a wide variety of fruits. Each household also tends to have some cattle, pigs, chickens, goats, and sheep.

The tales and other folklore of the Matengo have not been recorded as extensively as those of other ethnic groups. The earliest known recording of Matengo tales was done by Catholic missionaries. It is possible that some of what they recorded is still in manuscript form in the missionary archives in

Europe, but in 1908 Fr. Johannes P. Häfliger became the first person to publish Matengo folktales.[1]

Although there are many published collections of African folktales, there are not many studies of these folktales suitable for the average reader between high school and college. There is not yet a tradition of teaching and studying folktales. One of the causes for this is the lack of critical works on folktales suitable for the beginning student. This lack, in turn, has continued to reinforce the belief that folktales are not a subject worthy of serious study.

In writing this book, I have sought to share some thoughts about the nature of Matengo folktales. I invite you to think about what I say and about the tales; for these tales challenge us to think and explore themes and structures, just as literature does.

I recorded these tales in the early seventies with a cassette recorder. I did not then have professional training in folklore fieldwork. I was then developing a keen interest in folklore, especially folktales. It was only in later years that I got a better sense of how folklore fieldwork is done and documented.

"Hare and the Great Drought," "How Hare Helped Civet," and "What Hare Did To Lion and Hyena" were told by my late father, Mzee Leodgar Mbele, in our home at Lituru Village, with my mother, brothers and sisters as the audience. "Hare, Civet and Antelope" and "The Tale of Two Women" were told by my childhood friend Joseph Ndunguru, also of Lituru. Both of us were about twenty years old at the time. "The Tale of an Uncle and his Nephew" was told to me by my late brother, Kajanuka, of Mbinga, then in his mid-teens. He was visiting us at Lituru, and he

---

[1] Johannes P. Häfliger, "Fabeln der Matengo (Deutsch-Ostafrika)," *Anthropos*, III (1908), 244-247. The tales are in Matengo, with German transliterations.

told the tale there in my small bachelor house. The "Tale of Nokamboka" was told by Mrs. Kangologo of Lituru, at her house. She was a woman in her late twenties or early thirties. Her mother-in-law, her children, her neighbours' children, my friend Joseph Ndunguru, and I were present.

In the summer of 1977, I went to Litembo Primary school, in my home district of Mbinga, southern Tanzania, to collect folktales. I was able to get a number of pupils to tell tales. To ensure that the pupils would feel free and relaxed, I allowed them to go into a room all by themselves to tell the tales, recording them into my cassette recorder. I did not then realize that this prevented me from observing who was telling which tale and how. At that point, my own understanding of folklore fieldwork was rather rudimentary. But this is how I collected three tales in this collection: "Katigija," "Hawk and Crow," and "The Monster in the Rice Field." They were all told by school girls in the company of other school girls and boys. The other tales that were told on that occasion are not included here. I hope to translate them at a future date.

This book is not for specialists. It seeks to provide an introduction to Matengo folktales, using English translations of those tales. I hope to present a selection of Matengo tales in a proper scholarly format in the future.

Translating oral tales presents many problems. It is impossible to translate accurately what is expressed in a given language. There will always be differences between the original and the translation. The problem becomes more serious when the two languages are as far apart as Matengo and English, representing two very different cultures.

This problem is due not only to the fact that words in one language may not have equivalents in the other language. There is also the problem that sounds that have meaning in Matengo may not have meanings in English. There are also ideophones, which cannot be translated. One example that I find interesting, whenever I think about these problems, is the way different cultures represent the crowing of a cock. In English, the cock is supposed to crow: "Cock-a-doodle doo!" In Matengo, it is *"Ngou ka le kye ng'oo!"* Every language has its own rendering of this very well know phenomenon. When translating a Matengo folktale into English, I prefer keeping the Matengo form of such phenomena rather than the English form.

Matengo, like most languages of Tanzania, is not a written language. We do not have a standardized system for representing its sounds. This language has vowel sounds which do not exist in other African languages like Swahili. These required special symbols. Two sounds in particular need special attention. I have rendered them as "ou" and "ei," that are similar to the sounds in the English words "cope" and "cape," respectively.

Each tale in this book is accompanied by my comments. These comments are not meant to represent the way the Matengo interpret these tales, nor are they meant to convey what these tales may have meant at any time in their course of their existence. The comments are merely my personal response to the tales, my thoughts, and my impressions as I follow the tales. They are neither comprehensive nor final. There are many other things that I could have said about the form, content, and functions of these tales. You can and should be able to say a lot of things about these tales which I have omitted.

Some of the tales in this collection have been published. "The Story of an Uncle and His Nephew" appeared in *Umma*, the Journal of the Department of Literature, University of Dar es Salaam, vol. 5, 2 (1975), 92-96; "What Hare Did to Lion and Hyena" appeared in *Umma*, Vol. 6, 1 (1976), 80-82; "How Hare Helped Civet" was first published in *Earthwatch*, July/August (1993), 14-15.

In the course of my research, I received financial assistance from the Research and Publications Committee of the University of Dar es Salaam, and the German Academic Exchange Service (DAAD), which I gratefully acknowledge. I also wish to thank Professor Tonya Huber-Bowen of the University of Kansas, for taking an interest in some of the trickster tales in this collection and using them in her classes. My own students at St. Olaf College also inspired me by their response to the trickster tales I gave them to read in my Hero and Trickster course. I wish to acknowledge with much gratitude the assistance and hospitalily granted to me by the Matengo people. I have fond memories of the evenings when my late father, Mzee Leodgar Mbele, told us stories. I dedicate this book to him.

How Hare Helped Civet

Lion and Civet were great friends.

One day, Civet said to Lion:

"Look. It is true that we have a very good life. But there's one thing that we lack. And that's *cattle*! You know very well how important it is to own cattle. So let's go out and get some."

The two of them went out to look for cattle. Lion bought a bull, and Civet bought a cow. They returned home and started looking after their animals.

Time passed. The bull mounted the cow, and the cow became pregnant. Time passed. And the cow calved. When this happened, Civet was not around. Lion removed the calf from where the cow was and placed it where his bull was.

Soon after, Civet, who had gone to fetch water for his cow, came back with the water. Before Civet had set down his water, Lion ran up to him and with great excitement broke the news to him:

"Look!" he cried. "My animal has a calf!"

This sparked off a dispute between the two of them. Civet maintained that only his cow could have borne the calf, and that bulls never calved. And Lion insisted vehemently that it was his bull that had calved.

Now, as the two were thus quarreling, Hare passed by. And though he heard what they were quarreling about, he just went on his way, feeling pity for Civet.

When he came home, Hare began thinking how he could help Civet out of his predicament. At long last, he got an idea. He took his gourds and tied one at each end of a staff, and he promptly set off, carrying the staff on his shoulder.

On the way, he met Lion. Lion asked:

"How, now, Hare; where could you be going?"

Hare said:

"Oh, I'm just going down to the river nearby to fetch water for my father who is weak and in bed. He just gave birth to a baby."

Hearing this, Lion roared with laughter and told Hare to stop being foolish.

"How," Lion asked, "could your father have a baby?"

And Hare promptly answered:

"But you yourself are claiming that your bull calved!"

Suddenly enraged, Lion flew at Hare, and Hare threw away his gourds and took to his heels. With Lion chasing him, it was a matter of life and death for Hare, and he ran as he had never run in all his life.

At length, Hare saw a cave in the distance and decided to head towards it. Immediately he shot into the cave, he jumped up and held the roof of the cave, howling:

"Help! The cave is collapsing!"

And that same instant, Lion was already in the cave, and he, too, jumped up and helped to hold up the roof with all his strength.

"Now," Hare said, "hold on, otherwise the cave is going to crush both of us to death. I have an idea to lighten this task for both of us. I'll go and get some props to help us hold up the cave. Hold on tight!"

Lion stretched his muscles and pushed the roof of the cave up more firmly. Hare left Lion there, never to return.

For a whole week, Lion held up that rock, and, in the end, he died from exhaustion.

Hare came along and saw that Lion was dead. He set out looking for Civet, and when he met him, he invited him to see what had happened to Lion.

When Civet saw that Lion was dead, he rejoiced with all his heart, and thanked Hare very lavishly. And Hare told Civet to go his way and take the cattle with him, for they were now all his.

And that is how the tale ended.

How Hare Helped Civet

Short as it is, this tale contains a number of themes and raises significant issues. Among the themes are the trickster, friendship, and gender, as well as crime and punishment.

This is a trickster tale. It is, however, an unusual trickster tale: Hare, the trickster, uses his cleverness to help someone in distress. Typically, in Matengo and other African tales, the trickster is a mischief maker, out to create trouble for others. The Matengo trickster is hardly ever interested in helping anyone.

Although in this tale Hare does his tricks in order to help Civet, it is not easy to say that that is his sole or even main motive. When we consider what he says and does, we wonder whether his main purpose is to help Civet or to put Lion in trouble.

Among the issues the tale raises is that of gender and sexual roles. Lion and Civet argue over whether the cow or the bull gave birth to the calf. On the surface, this sounds like a trivial question, since we all know that the cow calved. However, it appears that the question goes deeper than that, since it forces us to consider the role of the male and the female in reproduction. Since the cow cannot reproduce without the bull and vice versa, it is not easy to say that the calf was produced by the cow. Lion's claim that his bull calved may sound absurd at first, but it is really no more absurd than Civet's claim.

The problem is that Lion does not think in this manner. He knew he was lying when he said his bull had calved. He did not believe his own words but only wanted to take advantage of Civet. If he believed that the male has a role in reproduction, and that it is not easy to say whether it is the male or the female that gives birth, he would not have become angry when Hare said his father had a baby.

Nor does Hare believe his own words that his father had a baby. He simply says this to provoke Lion and perhaps to force Lion to realize his own unfair treatment of Civet.

Lion is neither honest nor humble; he gets angry with Hare. Instead of seeing his own weakness and acknowledging his evil, he chooses to victimize Hare. Because of this, when Hare manages to punish Lion, we feel that he deserves that punishment.

As is the case with many folktales, this tale engages us in speculations about the possibility of males conceiving and having babies. This sounds fantastical, but it is an interesting question: suppose males could play the reproductive roles women play. What would happen if males could conceive and bear babies? The tale raises the possibility of reversing the male and female roles in reproduction.

In general, the trickster in many cultures is associated with such reversals. Often the trickster challenges the established social and natural order. The trickster's motives and actions often seek to reverse the order of things.

It might be a good idea to compare Civet, Lion and Hare, to determine which of them can be described with terms such as intelligent, stupid, evil, helpful, or mischievous. Try doing that. One good hint is that it is Civet who proposes the idea of buying cattle. He seems intelligent. What else can we say about him, and what can we say about Lion and Hare?

The role of trickster in this tale belongs to Hare. However, Lion attempts to play the role of trickster as well. He tricks Civet by claiming that his bull calved. The question remains, however, whether Lion actually tricked Civet or whether he got his way simply because he is stronger than Civet.

Hare, on the other hand, is indisputably a trickster. He uses his cunning to provoke Lion into anger and into his own doom. If we choose to consider Lion as somehow a trickster as well, we may consider him a trickster who finally got tricked.

Would you agree that the tale contains moral lessons? If so, what are these?

What is the identity of the characters in this tale? They look like animals, but are they? Lion and Civet are animal-like characters, but they are not animals. They behave like humans, going to the extent of buying and keeping cattle. The cattle in this tale are true animals. Hare is not the hare we see in the bush and eat; he is a unique creature who exists only in folktales.

In my comments, I have assumed that Lion and Civet are male. In the Matengo language, there is no indication whether the two are male or female. That is the nature of that language.

Hare, Civet, and Antelope

Once there was Hare and Civet. It came to pass that they made an agreement to be close friends. And from that day onward, Hare and Civet lived like the greatest friends.

One day, the two of them decided to go and feast themselves on groundnuts in a granary that was some distance away. So, Hare and Civet set out towards that granary. When they reached it, Clever Hare climbed in first. He stayed in there for a short while and then called his friend to join him. As soon as Civet was in the granary, the two fellows went on a munching spree, devouring the groundnuts.

The two chaps went on devouring those groundnuts for a long time. Then, as luck would have it, the owner of the granary appeared! Hearing noises in the granary, he suspected there was something fishy going on inside there. The man stood outside the granary and called out,

"Who are you, inside there!"

When they heard this, Hare and Civet paused and listened. Then Hare whispered to Civet,

"Tell him, 'It's I.'" And Civet promptly shouted, "It's I!"

"What are you doing there?" the man asked.

Hare whispered to Civet,

"Say, 'I'm eating groundnuts' "

And Civet told the man outside:

"I'm eating up the groundnuts."

As soon as Civet had said this, Hare told him:

"Pinch me!"

Civet pinched Hare, and Hare vanished!

The man got into the granary and caught Civet.

"Civet!" the man said, "what are you doing here?" His voice was threatening.

"Please," Civet pleaded, "I was with Hare."

"Where is Hare, then?" the man demanded.

"He escaped, leaving me here," explained Civet, trembling with fear.

The man was stern.

"Why did you let him go?" he demanded. "I have caught you," he went on solemnly, "and today you are going to repent!"

Hearing this, Civet began pleading for mercy. He pleaded and pleaded, making himself exceedingly pathetic. And his pains bore fruit!

"Go your way," the man said at last. "Go your way. I'll forget what has happened today. We'll catch Hare one of these days, though."

On being released, Civet sped out of sight.

*   *   *   *   *

Another day, Hare again told his friend Civet:

"Let's go and eat those groundnuts."

Civet promptly refused.

"Never again!" he said categorically. "You left me in trouble last time, and I'm not going again!"

"Let bygones be bygones," Hare pleaded. "Let's go eat those groundnuts."

At last Civet gave in. And they set out towards the granary. When they got inside the granary, they fell into their orgy, as usual.

As luck would have it, however, while the two fellows were working on the groundnuts, the man came! Hearing noises in the granary, he called out:

"Hey! Who are you, inside there?"

Hare whispered to Civet:
"Say, 'It's I.'"
Civet shouted to the man outside:
"It's *we*."
"What are you doing there?" the man asked.
Hare whispered to Civet:
"Say, 'I'm eating groundnuts!'"
Civet shouted:
"*We* are eating groundnuts!"

When Hare asked Civet to pinch him this time, it was too late for the man had already entered the granary. He caught the two of them, and he was taking them home.

On the way, Hare escaped. And the man vented his anger on Civet. He said:

"Last time I pardoned you. Yet you dared to repeat the offense. This time I'm going to deal with you mercilessly!"

It was clear to Civet that, this time, no amount of pleading would save him. He therefore meekly told the man:

"I'm at your mercy, and may your will prevail."

The man took Civet and killed him. He cut the corpse to pieces and threw the pieces away.

*   *   *   *   *

Hare was far from settled. His thirst for friends was egging him on, and he went and made another pact of friendship, this time with Antelope.

Antelope said to Hare:

"But I hear that Civet is dead. I'd like to believe that you are not leading me the same way."

With an assuring laugh, Hare shrugged off Antelope's fears:

"Trust me," he said. "I won't harm you. There's a great heap of groundnuts in that granary. Let's go eat them!"

So, they left for the granary. When they got inside it, Hare had some advice for his friend Antelope:

"A moment, please," he began. "We must work with care! The owner of the granary has a tendency to appear here in the most unexpected manner!"

With these wise words, the two fellows went to work. Antelope was simply amazed at the speed and thoroughness with which Hare was devouring the groundnuts.

Then, of course, the owner of the granary appeared!

"Hey!' he called. "Who are you, in there?"

Hare whispered to Antelope, instructing him to reply, "It's I."

"It's *we!*" Antelope shouted.

"What are you doing?" the man inquired.

Hare told Antelope to say, "I'm eating groundnuts."

"*We* are eating groundnuts!" Antelope told the man.

Hare escaped, and the man caught Antelope. The man spoke to Antelope angrily:

"I've suffered a great deal on account of the likes of you. First it was Hare and Civet. But Civet I killed. And now it is you, Antelope!"

Antelope was quite afraid.

"It's Hare's fault," he pleaded; "for it was he who led me into all this."

"We're not setting you free," said the man. "We must kill you."

And so, Antelope was killed. But they did not cut him to pieces. After they had skinned him and taken out his entrails, they dried him and then hung him from the ceiling, above the fireplace. There he dried up and became a very stiff mummy.

Now it happened that whenever the villagers had gone to work in their fields, the mummy got down from where it used to hang, went to the wells where the villagers fermented their maize, took out some of the maize and dried it, ready for pounding. Then it selected a healthy-looking cock, killed and cooked it. And so, every day, the mummy cooked itself plenty of *ugali*[2] and ate it together with the cock it had killed. After it had eaten its fill, the mummy would climb to the ceiling and place itself in the same hanging position as before.

Now, when the people returned from their fields they said:

"Oh! Look! The big cock is nowhere to be seen! Where has it gone?"

Then they resolved that someone must stay behind and keep watch.

On the first day, they told the old lady of the village to keep watch. So when everybody else went to the fields, the old lady remained behind.

The mummy got down, and dodging the old lady, it went to the wells, took out some two *debes*[3] of maize, dried and pounded it, and cooked some *ugali*. *Then* it caught a fat calf and killed it. After it had cooked the meat, the mummy spoke to the old lady:

"Old Lady, come let's eat *ugali*."

And so, Antelope fed the old lady with *ugali* till she was full up. And the mummy itself ate its fill.

---

[2] *Ugali* is a form of food made with maize flour. One boils water and puts the flour in it and stirs it until it hardens. Ugali is not eaten alone, but normally with beans, meat, fish, eggs, or cooked vegetables.

[3] A *debe* is a cubical tin can with a capacity of four gallons.

When the villagers come back in the evening, the mummy is up, hanging from the ceiling, as usual. When they ask:

"What's been happening, Grand Lady?" the old lady couldn't say anything palatable, except to mumble some words implying that she didn't know what had happened to the calf and the maize. The *ugali* she had eaten had gone right into her head!

The villagers told her that they thought she was not a suitable look-out, and they suggested that the old man of the village should have a try at the task.

So, the old man remained behind and kept watch. The mummy got down, picked its way to the wells and got itself some five *debes* of maize.

When it came back it pounded the maize and, going among the cattle, it picked a big bull and killed it. After the mummy had prepared the food, it called the old man:

"Old Man, come let's eat."

Very thankfully and with a great appetite, the old man sat down to eat the delicious meal. He ate and ate and ate. The mummy asked:

"How, now, Grandpa, have you eaten your fill?"

"Not yet," said the old man. And so, he ate and ate and ate. The two of them ate up everything, to the smallest crumb. When they finish eating, the mummy goes up to its place under the ceiling.

When the villagers returned in the evening, they asked the old man:

"Our Old Man, how was the watch?"

The old man didn't say anything satisfactory. He just mumbled that he didn't know what had happened. This was all because of the mummy's meal. The *ugali* had clearly gone into the old man's head!

The villagers dismissed the old man, saying:

"You, too, are quite worthless. Our things continue to disappear because of the likes of you. We can't rely on you any more. Today, I'll keep watch myself."

So, the man of the house took charge of the watch. The mummy got down and did all it used to do, unaware that it was being watched.

When it was discovered that all the loss in the village had been caused by the mummy, they decided that it was high time the mummy was eaten. So, they set about cutting the mummy up, ready for cooking. But, strangely, though the thing had hung over the fireplace for a very long time and had now become dry and stiff, when they cut it up, it shed blood! Nobody could tell how such a thing could happen, nor where the blood came from!

After they had cooked the meat, they began to eat it. Now, it happened that every person who ate a piece of the meat, a bird escaped from their backside. Everybody who ate a piece of the meat, no matter how small, a bird escaped from their backside!

Now, the birds flew away. They flew and flew and flew, until, at last, they came to a certain person's house. They landed on the threshold of that house. After they had landed, the owner of the house said to the others:

"Look! There are birds here!"

He picked up a stone and killed one of the birds with it. The other birds flew away. They flew and flew and flew, until they disappeared behind a mountain.

Now, the people of that house took the dead bird and roasted it, with a view to eating it. Now each person who tasted a piece of that bird, a bird escaped from their backside. And all those birds flew away. They flew and flew and disappeared behind the

mountain where the other birds had gone, that being
the end of the tale.

Comments on
Hare, Civet, and Antelope

There are some cultural elements in this tale that I need to explain. The Matengo, like other African people, venerate the elders. Considered wise and responsible, the elders are the ones who make decisions and offer advice and guidance.

In this tale, we have the old lady and the old man, who take part in guarding the homestead. The tale presents them as behaving in a manner that is not appropriate for elders. They abandon their responsibility as elders and care more about the meals cooked by the mummy. This aspect of the tale is somehow funny, but it is also disturbing.

The tale criticizes the two elders. This is a serious issue. In Matengo and other African societies, elders can only be criticized by other elders. In this way, the tale crosses a delicate line in matters of decorum. The fact that this tale is told even by youths highlights this problem. When the tale is told by young people or to young people, it does raise the disturbing prospect of the violation of a taboo. Children and youths have to show great respect for elders, and they should not be in a situation such as this where they laugh at elders.

The elders are called respectively *Ambujamundu* and *Ahokomundu*. The first term means "grandmother of someone" and "grandmother" simultaneously. The second one means "grandfather of someone" or "grandfather," simultaneously.

The Matengo word for mummy is *"kipeika."* (pronounce the "ei" like the "a" in lazy). The Matengo commonly hang meat from the ceiling or rafters above the fireplace. The smoke and heat both dry and preserve the meat.

On several occasions the narrator, Kajanuka, switched tenses, as is shown in the text. When he recounted the capture of Antelope, he made the owner of the granary speak in the plural form: "We are not setting you free...We must kill you." The effect of this is to indicate that the man was not representing himself but his family and even his village. All these shifts give us a sense of Kajanuka's narrative style.

The friendship between Hare and Civet, and between Hare and Antelope, is interesting. In each case, the first act or expression of friendship is to go and steal groundnuts. We expect friends to do positive things together. Then, as soon as the owner of the groundnuts discovers the two friends in the granary, Hare abandons his friends, leaving them in the granary to face the music. Africans know that any friendship involving a trickster cannot be true friendship.

Civet gets into a friendship with Hare two times. The first time, he is caught by the owner of the granary; the second time he is killed. Consider carefully Civet's words and actions on both occasions. Did he learn anything the first time? Why did he trust Hare the second time?

Civet failed to learn the most important lesson of all, that no one should accept Hare's offer of friendship. This failure costs Civet his life.

As Civet goes, Antelope comes in. Antelope seems a little more intelligent than Civet. He has heard that Civet died, and that Hare was connected with that sad event. Consider carefully how he questions Hare. Consider how he behaves in the granary. Is Antelope intelligent enough?

I think that the trouble with Antelope is that he is satisfied with mere verbal assurances from Hare. This weakness costs him his life.

Civet and Antelope make bad decisions, and they pay for the mistake with their own lives. However, Antelope is different from Civet. After being killed and eaten by the villagers, he changes into birds. In other words, he continues to live. In many African folktales, we come across creatures, especially birds, whose life cannot be ended completely. After being killed, they either come back to life again or change into something that continues to live, such as the birds in this story.

Such creatures often appear in connection with crimes. They witness a crime, and the criminal kills them so that they might not tell people about the crime, but the creatures come back to life. The cycle of killing and resurrection continues until, finally, the creature manages to reveal information about the crime, leading to the punishment of the criminal.

There are four main characters in this tale, Hare, Civet, Antelope and the man. Are the first three animals? This is an interesting question. One can say that Hare, Civet and Antelope are animals, but they represent human qualities. They behave like human beings: they form friendships, they talk, they set out with the intention of stealing groundnuts. Animals do not steal, they just go and eat whatever they find. If these three were real animals, they would not know they were going to steal groundnuts.

What is even more important is that in the Matengo language, these folktale characters have names that distinguish them from the animals that we know as hare, civet and antelope. The folktale character, Hare, is called *Kapesa* in Matengo. The animal that we call a hare or a rabbit is called *kipesa*. Similarly, the folktale character Civet is called *Nahungu*, in Matengo, while the animal that we call the civet is called *lihungu*. As a folktale character, Antelope is known as *Nahoulouku*, while the animal that we know as the antelope is called *houlouku*.

Nevertheless, we cannot say that this is all. These creatures are often ambiguous, being animals or animal-like in some situations or some ways, and something else in other situations or ways. Antelope is killed and eaten by the villagers, just like any antelope. Still, the miracles that Antelope performs after being killed show that he is not a normal antelope but a creature of the imagination. The calves and cocks that Antelope kills are true animals, it seems. The lesson to learn here is that we have to be careful when we discuss these folktale creatures.

There is the man in this tale. What kind of person is he? Can we discuss his behaviour? Is he kind or cruel? Do you sympathize with him or do you sympathize with Civet, Hare, and Antelope? When I consider that this man worked hard to grow and harvest the groundnuts, I feel that he has the right to be angry with the thieves and to punish them.

There are aspects of this tale that we can call fantastic. Hare escapes from the granary by merely being pinched. The mummy, dry as it is, bleeds when it is cut into pieces. Every piece of the mummy's meat that is eaten by the villagers changes into a bird. All these are fantastic elements.

The idea of fantastic elements in folktales raises problems. Did the people who created these tales consider these elements fantastic? Perhaps it is only we, the people of today, who consider these elements fantastic. The people of the past, and indeed many people today, believe in witchcraft, for example, which involves many things which are truly strange or supernatural. For such people, the things that happen in this tale are real, not fantastic. All this complicates the question of the fantastic dimension in folktales. What do you think?

In any case, the method by which Hare escapes from the granary, and the method by which Antelope escapes from the villagers' stomachs are interesting. They are techniques that the story uses to solve particular problems. Hare is trapped in the granary, just as Antelope is trapped in the villagers' stomachs. How does the story proceed from there? How do these two characters escape? The story must provide a technical solution to this problem, so that the story can move on. To solve this problem, the story resorts to what we call the fantastic element.

The idea of the trickster permeates this tale. It is, in fact, the foundation of the tale. Hare is the first trickster we encounter, as he sets about establishing friendships and getting his friends into trouble. They are the dupes.

Antelope, however, has a double character. He is Hare's dupe when he is alive, but after he is killed and turned into a mummy, he becomes a trickster. He is able to consume the food and livestock in the village without being found out for a long time. He manages to avoid being caught by feeding the guards with delicious meals. Finally, when he is cut into pieces, cooked, and eaten, he is able to change into birds and escape.

One of the important themes that the tale deals with is that of duty. We have several characters here who fail in their duties. The elders fail in their duties, as I have said, and other characters do so, too. They fall prey to bribery. The tale thus highlights universal human problems.

What Hare Did to Lion and Hyena

Walking along the road one day, Hare saw Lion and his wife by the roadside. They were eating meat, as is their custom.

"Friends," Hare remarked, "what a pity that you eat your meat raw!"

Lion said, "We always eat our meat raw. What else can we do?"

"Poor fellows!" Hare said. "Meat eaten raw is not good at all! You got to roast it to know how tasty meat can be!"

When they heard this, Lion and his wife asked Hare to roast some of the meat for them so they could ascertain the truth of this words.

Hare took the meat and roasted it. Then he gave it to them to taste. When Lion and his wife tasted it, they swore they had never eaten such tasty meat before. And they deeply regretted that all their lives they had eaten raw meat.

"Now," they told Hare, "you will work for us as meat roaster. We shall pay you accordingly."

Hare accepted the job, but he made one request.

"Let us be clear on one thing," he said. "When I have roasted the meat, I will not feed you with my bare hands. I'm afraid of your teeth! Instead, I will use tongs to throw the meat to you, and you will have to catch it."

Lion and his wife agreed to this request, and off into the bush they went to hunt animals.

Hare set about collecting firewood and made a fire. When, in the evening, the Lions came with the meat, Hare roasted it, and using the tongs, he threw it to them to eat.

Things went on this way for a number of days. Then, one day, Hare saw that the Lions had brought a great quantity of meat. He set about roasting it, as was his custom. Then he took two sizeable stones and put them in the fire, together with the meat. He added firewood to the fire and poked it to make sure that the meat was roasting well. The meat sizzled as the fat streamed from it, bathing the stones until they looked as tempting as well-roasted chunks of meat.

In the evening, when the Lions came for their supper, Hare took a chunk of meat and threw it to them. They ate it. Hare bent down again to pick up another piece of meat. He threw it to the Lions and they ate it. Then Hare picked up one of the stones and threw it to Lion. Lion caught it with his mouth and as it was terribly hot, he swallowed it fast and dropped down dead.

Hare said scornfully:

"Look! The fool doesn't know how to catch meat! You surely can do better than him," he added, turning to Lion's wife.

Then Hare picked up the second stone with his tongs and threw it to her. She, too, swallowed it and fell down dead.

When Hare saw what he had done, he laughed:

"Don't pretend to be dead. That was only meat!"

Hare moved to where the Lions were lying and shook them a little. They were indeed dead. Hare then set about skinning them. When he finished this work, he took the skins and filled them with grass. Then he sewed them up so that they looked like real lions again. When he had finished doing this, he put the "lions" away and sat down to roast and eat the meat the Lions had brought, throwing the bones all over the place.

Then, Hyena came along.

"Hare," he called, "will you object to my picking up these bones?"

"Bones only?" Hare asked. "I won't care a bit. Help yourself!"

Hyena fell upon the bones and started feasting.

Some time afterwards, Hare asked:

"Hyena, will you object to my playing with your tail?"

"My tail?" Hyena asked. "Go ahead. I don't mind."

Hare began playing with hyena's tail, and he went and took one end of a rope which he had tied to the neck of one of the "lions" and came and tied it to Hyena's tail.

Then, while Hyena was very busy crunching and swallowing the bones, Hare told him:

"Friend, while you are eating those bones you would do well to turn around and see the owner."

Hyena ignored these words, saying:

"What are you talking about! Who else owns these bones apart from you? All I know is that you are the owner."

"Please," Hare insisted, "do look behind you and see the owner."

Hyena turned round and saw "Lion" gazing at him. Did Hyena stay there another second? He took off like lightning!

As he was tearing through the bush, he turned round from time to time, only to see the "lion" hot at his heels, and it looked as if the "lion" was catching up with him! Hyena strained his muscles and ran even faster, but each time he turned to look back, the "lion" was just about to catch him!

The chase headed towards Hyena's cave. When they got there, Hyena shot into the cave, but when he turned round he saw the "lion" blocking the doorway, his fierce eyes staring into the cave. It became clear to Hyena, now, that a great tragedy had befallen him and his family.

Hyena and his family stayed indoors that whole week. The "lion" was still standing in the doorway, and there was no sign that it would leave. Another week went by, and the "lion" was still there in the doorway.

Hyena and his wife told each other that matters were so bad that hunger was going to kill them all. So, they decided to kill one of their children, and they ate him. A week passed. They killed another child and ate him. Yet another week went by. They ate the third child. The "lion" was still there in the doorway. There was no more child left.

Hyena, at long last, said to his wife:

"My wife, cut your tail so we can eat it."

The tail was cut and eaten.

Another day Hyena said to his wife:

"Cut your ears so we can eat them."

The ears were cut and eaten.

The "lion," however, was still in the doorway.

One day Hyena said:

"Let us wrestle. Whoever is thrown down should be eaten by the other."

They started wrestling, and instantly Hyena was flat on the ground.

"No!" he roared. "We've wrestled like women! Let's start again."

And so, they began wrestling again. This time the wife was thrown down. She protested:

"That can't be! We've wrestled like women! I had not stood properly."

But Hyena shouted triumphantly:

"Not at all! We agreed that whoever is thrown down shall be eaten."

So, Hyena killed his wife and ate her.

But it was not long before Hyena began to feel hungry again. Now, there was completely nothing to eat, and the "lion" was still in the doorway. Hyena sat down and thought things over.

"What a calamity!" he said. "Suppose I cut my tail and eat it. Then, my ears. Then what? What will remain of my body except a shapeless monstrosity? It is better that I should be eaten by this lion than to deform myself that way."

An idea occurred to him, then. He picked up two sizable pieces of firewood from the fireplace and made for the door. Gathering all his strength, he flung one of them at the "lion." The "lion" fell backwards and landed outside!

Hyena went out to inspect it, and he discovered that it was no lion at all, but merely lion's skin stuffed with grass! Hyena was very sad indeed.

"What a calamity!" he cried. "What a great loss. What shall I do now?"

Hyena went and sat on a rock nearby and began mourning the loss of his family.

While Hyena was thus weeping on that rock, Hare passed along the road. When he saw Hyena, Hare called out a greeting to him. Hyena did not answer anything. Hare repeated his greeting, but Hyena kept quiet.

Then Hare said:

"My friend, let us call off this friendship of ours!"

And that is the end of the tale.

Comments on
What Hare Did to Lion and Hyena

This is a trickster tale, and Hare plays his usual role as trickster. The other characters—Lion, Lion's wife, and Hyena—are the dupes. A dupe is a character that is tricked.

One question is, did Hare accept the job because he wanted work or because he wanted a chance to do some mischief?

As is usual in Matengo folktales, Hyena has the tendency to turn up wherever there is a supply of bones. The appearance of Hyena in this tale marks the beginning of what we can consider a tale within the tale. Hyena's appetite for bones sets off a chain of events that leads to his having to stay indoors for a very long time, subsisting on the flesh of his own children and wife.

Consider the theme of food in this tale. The tale deals with this theme at length, starting with famine, which is the absence of food. It also deals with the question of what is proper food and what is not. At the beginning, the tale introduces the idea of raw meat. Hare says that it is not proper to eat raw meat, that meat should be roasted. The distinction between what is raw and what is cooked is strong in various cultures and is often surrounded by taboos. Food is not a simple matter; each culture has its own concept of what is edible and what is not, and the differences are often striking.

This tale gives some indication of different food customs and eating habits. In addition to the Lions' practice of eating raw meat, the tale presents Hyena, who eats bones, a peculiar kind of food because bones are left-overs. Nobody else eats bones. Then, when Hyena and his wife get hungry in their cave, they decide to eat their own children. This is a shocking idea because children are not food. The idea of eating each other's body parts is shocking, too. The tale makes us think about cannibalism.

The idea of cannibalism due to famine is not far fetched; again and again, there have been instances of cannibalism in various parts of the world under conditions of famine. Famine has also caused people to eat things they would normally not eat, such as various animals, insects, or plants.

The tale deals with the subject of male-female relationships, through its representation of the relationship between Hyena and his wife. This is a relationship of inequality and oppression, maintained and legitimized by the ideology of male supremacy. This ideology is summed up in the tale by the memorable phrase, "we've wrestled like women!" This phrase underlines the belief that women are not as good or as capable as men.

One of the tragic facts is that Hyena's wife objects to the outcome of the second wrestling match with the same phrase, "we've wrestled like women!" This shows how members of the oppressed sex can assimilate the ideology of oppression and thus perpetuate that oppression. This tale carries a profound insight into the dynamics of women's oppression.

The way Hyena is depicted in his role as husband is interesting. He is a selfish husband who oppresses his wife. He denies her her right to eat him after she has thrown him down. In this way, the tale points to the issue of man's many injustices towards woman. Now this is quite interesting, considering that the tale flourished in a male-centered society in which man's dominance was taken for granted and was one of the pillars of the social system. Yet in the same society, we encounter this tale which is so obviously critical of this vital aspect of the society. How do we explain this contradiction?

This contradiction should remind us of the need to think more critically than we normally do about the relationship between tales and social realities. We should not assume that tales always reflect or reinforce social realities; they can also question or contradict those realities.

In the end, we see Hyena mourning the loss of his children and wife. He refuses to respond to Hare's greeting because, in light of what has happened, the greeting amounts to adding insult to injury. One question remains: is Hyena being punished in this tale because of his greed for bones or because of Hare's cruelty?

Hare and the Great Drought

Long, long ago, over a certain land, there descended a great drought. And all the animals realized that they were in very serious trouble. So, they called a meeting to see what they could do. All the animals attended that meeting except Hare.

After some deliberation, the meeting resolved that they had to dig a well if they were to beat the drought at all. And so, in unison, they started digging a well. Then, the water came out and filled the well. And so it was that every time the animals returned from the wilderness where they were eating grass they came to the well to have a drink of water.

Then, one day, the animals resolved to post a guard at the well to prevent Hare from drawing water, for he was cunning and lazy. They appointed Tortoise guard. So, Tortoise took up his position and began guarding the well.

In the middle of the night, Hare came to the well to draw water. He was carrying some honey in a gourd. When he approached the well, he started singing:

Su-mpoumbi kunoga
Su-mpoumbi kunoga
Ku-ba kwabatibatibaki, nga-bi nabatibatibaki;
Su-mpoumbi kunoga
Su-mpoumbi kunoga
Ku-ba kwabatibatibaki, nga-bi nabatibatibaki.

A mysterious thing—how sweet

A mysterious thing—how sweet
If I had the chance
I would have mixed him some
A mysterious thing—how sweet
A mysterious thing—how sweet
If I had the chance
I would have mixed him some

Tortoise came out. Hare brought out some of the honey on a stalk of elephant grass. He gave it to Tortoise to taste.

"Hare!" exclaimed Tortoise, "It's really sweet!"

And Hare replied: "Don't mind. Sit down and eat as much of it as you want."

Then, as Tortoise was eating the honey, Hare went into the well, filled his two gourds with water and put them aside, outside the well. Then he went into the well again and bathed thoroughly. Finally he came out, took his gourds, and left for home. Tortoise remained behind, guarding the well.

In the morning, the animals came to the well to drink.

"Tortoise," they asked, "how come the water is so dirty? Who polluted it?"

"Honestly," swore Tortoise, "I don't know who did that. I was asleep."

In saying this, Tortoise was afraid of mentioning Hare, knowing that if he did, he would surely miss the sweet honey when Hare came to the well again.

Anyhow, the animals drank the water, dirty as it was. But as they were going back to graze, they said to one another:

"Friends, we must have another guard."

They appointed Crab their next guard.

Crab went into the well. And later, Hare came, singing his song:

Su-mpoumbi kunoga
Su-mpoumbi kunoga
Ku-ba kwabatibatibaki, nga-bi nabatibatibaki:
Su-mpoumbi kunoga
Su-mpoumbi kunoga
Ku-ba kwabatibatibaki, nga-bi nabatibatibaki.

A mysterious thing—how sweet
A mysterious thing—how sweet
If I had the chance, I would have mixed him
  some
A mysterious thing—how sweet
A mysterious thing—how sweet
If I had the chance, I would have mixed him
  some.

Crab was quiet and didn't even stir where he was. Hare sang again. But Crab remained still and quiet.

"Today they're dull," Hare boasted to himself, referring to the animals.

Then he went into the well and drew the water he needed. Crab remained still and quiet. Hare went into the well again to bathe. Then, Crab acted—he seized Hare's leg with an iron grip, and much as Hare struggled to free himself, much as he pleaded for release, Crab did not let go of Hare's leg, until morning, when the animals came. Then Crab announced to them all:

"Here's the culprit; I have caught him!"

The animals sat down to discuss how to punish Hare. At last, they decided to kill and eat him. Then, at this point, Hare spoke:

"Poor fellows," he said, "how futile for all of you to eat a small creature like me! Surely, after eating me you won't feel like having tasted anything at all. If you really want to have enough to eat out of me, I'll tell you what to do. Tie me to a tree overnight. I assure you that when you come back in the morning you will find me many times bigger than I am now—perhaps bigger than you, Elephant, there."

The animals looked for a rope, and then tied Hare to a tree. Then they left.

At night, Hyena came where Hare was.

"Hare," he said, "how come you are tied to that tree?"

"You won't believe it!" Hare said. "They've tied me here in order to kill an ox for me tomorrow. But, as you well know, friend, I don't have the proper teeth for such a job. And this is what is worrying me now. Look into my mouth and see for yourself."

With these words, Hare opened his mouth wide and Hyena had a good look into it.

Hyena laughed when he saw those teeth and said:

"Indeed, these can't be called teeth by any means."

And Hare replied:

"Now let's see yours."

And Hyena opened his big mouth wide. Hare looked into Hyena's mouth and what enormous teeth he saw there!

"You see!" Hare exclaimed. "How about untying me and tying you here so you can eat this whole ox with your powerful teeth?"

Hyena was very delighted. He promptly untied Hare, and Hare tied him to the tree. This done, Hare left.

As Hare was leaving, however, drums throbbed in the distance, accompanied by singing:

> *Ndi! Ndi! Ndi!*
> *Ndi! Ndi! Ndi!*
> *Lelenu kunkoma Kapesa!*

Ndi! Ndi! Ndi!
Ndi! Ndi! Ndi!
Lelenu kunkoma Kapesa!

Ndi! Ndi! Ndi!
Ndi! Ndi! Ndi!
Today, it is the killing of Hare!
Ndi! Ndi! Ndi!
Ndi! Ndi! Ndi!
Today, it is the killing of Hare!

It was the animals coming! Hyena became nervous.

"Hare!" he called, "but they're saying 'Today we're going to kill Hare'!"

Whereupon Hare answered:

"Really, I can't stand this any more. If you insist on trusting your unreasonable fears, let me untie you and you can tie me there. I'm so fed up with your baseless fears that I'd rather go and eat this meat, toothless as I am. Surely, if I can't chew it, I'm not so helpless as to fail to swallow it unchewed. I'm totally disappointed with you, Hyena!"

On hearing this threatening words, Hyena apologized to Hare and said:

"Cool down, please. Leave me here for a while."

And then, morning came. The drums were throbbing just nearby:

Ndi! Ndi! Ndi!
Lelenu kunkoma Kapesa!
Ndi! Ndi! Ndi!
Lelenu kunkoma Kapesa!

Ndi! Ndi! Ndi!
Today it is the killing of Hare!
Ndi! Ndi! Ndi!

Today, it is the killing of Hare!

Hare ran away.

The animals appeared and said to one another:

"Look! What did Hare say? He has grown so big, just as he said!"

So the animals set about untying Hyena from the tree.

Hyena pleaded:

"Friends, I'm not the one you want."

The animals did not listen to his words. They killed him, divided his flesh among themselves, and ate it.

After all this, Hare appeared. He said:

"Friends, give me these bones you have thrown about, please. I don't need the meat."

The animals allowed Hare to take the bones. Hare collected those bones and left. He went and made a xylophone out of the bones. In no time, Hare's music became the talk of the whole land:

Nduli, ndulinduli, nduli, ndulinduli
Nu-ulombilombi wangu mee!
Nduli, ndulinduli, nduli, ndulinduli
Nu-ulombilombi wangu mee,
A-mba muja Kapesa mee,
Nalijembe pa-tumba mee
Pa-tumba naliboleli mee
Ka-be mee!
Ka-be mee!

Nduli, ndulinduli, nduli, ndulinduli
Nu-ulombilombi wangu mee!
Nduli, ndulinduli, nduli, ndulinduli
Nu-ulombilombi wangu mee,
A-mba muja Kapesa mee,
Nalijembe pa-tumba mee

Pa-tumba naliboleli mee
Ka-be mee!
Ka-be mee!

When Crow heard this song, he was moved with envy, and he swooped down and grabbed the xylophone and flew with it into the air. Hare grabbed a piece of flaming firewood and flung it at Crow, knocking him so seriously that he let go the xylophone. Crow was defeated for the day.

So, Crow went and told Thunder:

"Have you heard how famous Hare has become, with his xylophone?"

Thunder came down and grabbed the xylophone from Hare and flew back to his home, up in the sky. When he came home, he put the xylophone aside.

Down here on earth, Hare was thinking:

"Oh! Poor me. Now that Thunder has taken my xylophone, how can I get it back? Where he stays is too far away—up in the sky...Anyhow, it doesn't matter. I know that these days Thunder is gathering grass near here to thatch his house. I'll get him."

So, Hare left and went to the place where Thunder had collected his bundles of thatch. He looked for the biggest bundle of them all, knowing that Thunder had already started taking those bundles to his home in the sky, and he went and hid himself in that bundle.

Thunder's wife came and carried the bundles of grass to the sky, one after the other.

Finally, there remained only the biggest bundle, which she found too heavy for her. She went home and told Thunder that she had carried all the bundles except one, which was too heavy for her.

Thunder said:

"It's quite likely that I made that one bigger than the others."

So, Thunder came down and picked up that bundle and, arriving home, he set it down beside the others. This done, he and his wife went into their house.

Hare got out of the bundle of grass and went to sit at the *sengu*.

When Thunder came out, he saw Hare sitting at the *sengu*, and he greeted him at once:

"How are you, Friend."

"I'm fine," said Hare.

"When did you come?" asked Thunder.

"Just now," Hare said.

"I've also just come from down there," said Thunder. "I was collecting grass."

"Ooh!" Hare put in. "We've come one close after the other. You were just ahead of me."

The two of them sat down and began talking, until evening came. Then they said:

"Let's go to sleep."

Hare said:

"I'll be grateful if I could sleep in the old woman's, that is, your mother's house."

Hare made this request on purpose. He knew that Thunder used to keep the night in the house of the old woman. The night was being kept in a pot, and it was necessary that always at dawn the pot should be opened, or else the day would not break.

Hare went and slept in the old woman's house. In the middle of the night, he removed the lid from the pot, took out the night, and came with it down to earth, leaving Thunder with the xylophone.

When it was about time for daybreak, Thunder called out:

"Grandlady! Grandlady! Will you please release the night; the morning is late in coming."

The old woman got up. When she uncovered the pot, she discovered that the night was not there.

"Thunder!" she called, "the night's missing from the pot!"

"Where's it?" Thunder called back.

"It's nowhere to be seen," said the old woman, "and the pot is empty!"

Thunder asked:

"Is Hare there?"

"He's not here," said the old woman. "He's gone!"

"Then," said Thunder, "it's quite likely that he's taken the night away. I'll have to follow him, although it is still dark."

Then, Thunder came down from the sky, carrying Hare's xylophone. When he came down, he gave Hare his xylophone, and Hare gave him back his night, which he took back to the sky. Thunder stayed in peace up there, and Hare stayed in peace down here with his xylophone. That is the end of the tale.

Comments on
Hare and the
Great Drought

The way the inhabitants of this land come together to discuss and solve their common problem is significant. It shows their communal spirit and life style. They believe in working together for the common good, and everybody is expected to act this way. Hare's refusal to follow this custom makes him a criminal. That is why the animals seek ways to punish him.

One problem with this tale is that Hare, the criminal, does not get punished. Through cunning, he manages not only to evade punishment, but also to have someone else, Hyena, receive the punishment. This is not just. As we read this tale, we may have expected what is called poetic justice, which means the bad characters being punished and the good or innocent being rewarded or vindicated. This tale lets us down. Perhaps it forces us to think.

Some questions arise from this. How did the animals fail to recognize Hyena, mistaking him for Hare? Then, when Hare appeared and asked for the bones, how did the animals fail to recognize him as the criminal they were looking for?

Such elements, which seem illogical to us, are common in folktales. Scholars call them narrative inconsistencies. We cannot always tell why tales contain such elements. Sometimes it is because the storyteller forgets something in the tale or mixes up things without intending to do so.

Sometimes narrative inconsistencies exist because the focus of the storyteller and the audience is elsewhere. When a story is told to an audience, it is an overwhelming, complex experience, involving song, body movement, audience participation, and it may move rather fast, so that there is no time to notice the inconsistencies. The storyteller and the audience are swept by the tempo and excitement of the performance and have not time or motivation to pay attention to the details of what we might call the logic of the plot. Since we are reading the story as a text, we can go through it slowly, back and forth, and are thus more able to notice inconsistencies.

We can discuss the songs in the tale. There is first the song which Hare sings to lure the guards out of the well. The song is difficult to translate. It is deliberately suggestive and even obscure, because Hare wants it to arouse the curiosity of the guards, to fascinate and tempt them and lure them out of the well. However the general meaning of the song could be rendered as follows:

> *Sumpoumbi*! how sweet it is!
> *Sumpoumbi*! how sweet it is!
> If I had the chance
> I would have mixed him some

We don't really know what *sumpoumbi* is, but in this tale, it is supposed to be something fascinating and tempting, like honey. Hare provides a useful hint when he says it is sweet. We, the audience, are lucky that we have been told that it is honey, but the poor guards in the well have no idea what this sweet thing, *sumpoumbi*, really is. No wonder they cannot resist the temptation to come out and taste it. Hare says, in this song, that he is carrying this sweet thing and he would be willing to prepare some for a vaguely defined "someone." In my translation, I have used the word "him," but in Matengo there is no gender marker, and a more accurate translation would be simply "someone." In referring to "someone," Hare has in mind the person who might be in the vicinity guarding the well. Hare is almost certain that there is a guard somewhere; but he does not know the exact details. He thus sings his song as a trap in an effort to find out.

The second song is actually a chant, accompanied by the sound of drums, *ndi! ndi! ndi!* The chant simply says: "Today we are killing Hare."

The final song is sung by Hare, after he has made his xylophone. The words *Nduli, ndulinduli nduli, ndulinduli,* are imitations of the musical sounds of the xylophone. The song can be translated as follows:

> *Nduli, ndulinduli nduli, ndulinduli*
> I and my xylophone, yeah
> *Nduli, ndulinduli nduli, ndulinduli*
> I and my xylophone, yeah
> Given to me by the Noble Hare, yeah
> So I could sing away at a secluded bushy place, yeah
> A suitable bushy place I grew used to, yeah!
> Again yeah!
> Again yeah!

The phrase I have used, "secluded bushy place," does not quite capture the meaning of the word *patumba*. The word evokes and connotes things which are not quite identifiable. But a little bush seems to me part of the meaning of the word.

Scholars tend to assume that the songs we see in folktales are very old. This idea is supported by the archaic words we often encounter in these songs. Word such as *sumpoumbi* and *patumba* are not common in Matengo; they could be archaic. Perhaps, in the past, people understood these words without any problems, but the language has changed. Being rhythmical and melodious, songs are easy to remember and transmit from one generation to the next. For the same reasons they are difficult to change. They thus tend to remain stable across time, unlike the other parts of the tales. This is why scholars think that the songs are the oldest elements in the tales.

In this tale, we encounter many characters. We also encounter the problem of whether these are animal characters or human characters in disguise. We see these characters discussing the problem of drought, and this shows that they are human-like. Similarly, Hare and Hyena talk about having an ox killed for them. In that context, Hare and Hyena assume human characteristics, and only the ox is a real animal. The tale blurs the boundary between the human and animal world, or, at least, it renders the boundary permeable.

This tale is significant in the way it comments about social life. In this community, it is expected that each individual works for the common good. Laziness and selfishness are not tolerated.

The tale describes bribery. That is what Hare is doing. Although Hare is shown as a bad character, an antisocial character, he is also capable of drawing our sympathy as he sits helpless after his xylophone has been taken away by Thunder. Hare is also charming when he sings his great song. In the original Matengo, this song is very pleasant.

Take some time to think about he characters in this tale. Are the guards good or bad? Do you blame them for failing in their duties or do you blame Hare?

What about Crow and Thunder? Do you think they are right in taking Hare's xylophone? What about Thunder's mother? Would you say that she failed in her duties just like the guards of the well?

Hare appears here in his classic role as trickster. He uses cunning to get what he did not work for and to avoid punishment. The strategy he uses to get water is very clever. The song he sings as he approaches the well is cleverly crafted to mesmerize the guards and lure them out.

Nevertheless, Hare is selfish and irresponsible; he does not want to work for the common good. He wants to exploit the labour of others. He viciously gets an innocent character, Hyena, to be killed for nothing; however, in Matengo culture, Hyena is not entirely innocent because he is known to be a stupid character who cannot control his appetite for bones. The Matengo do not really pity Hyena when he gets into trouble the way he does in this tale. He is, in a way, paying for his own weaknesses.

Although it is often difficult to say whether characters that appear in tales such as this one are animals or not, the characters in this tale are called *inyama*, a word that means animals. When the storyteller starts the tale, he or she says that all the *inyama* got together and decided to dig a well. That is why I have taken the liberty of referring to them as animals as well. However, the animals in this tale do represent human beings, giving the tale the quality of a fable.

Hawk and Crow

There was Hawk and Crow. Hawk said:
"Crow, let's go to lay eggs."
They went out and laid eggs. Then Hawk said:
"Crow, stay with the chicks. I'm going to fish."
Crow stayed.

When Hawk was gone, Crow ran away with the chicks.

Hawk fished, then came back. She looked everywhere, but she saw neither Crow nor the chicks. She set out looking for them.

She came to a house. She asked:
"Please, have you, by any chance, seen Crow pass this way?"

They said:
"She passed here; she was going to the river to feed her chicks with *ngoko*.[4] Hawk went behind the house and sang:

> *Mwakanakoungou malangu nzeilalei*
> *Malangu nzeilalei nzeilalei nzeilalei*
> *Mwakanakoungou malangu nzeilalei*
> *Malangu nzeilalei nzeilalei nzeilalei*
> *Mwakanitole banangu nzeilalei*
> *Banangu nzeilalei nzeilalei nzeilalei*

> You, Crows, you've no brains,
> No brains, no brains, no brains.
> You, Crows, you've no brains,
> No brains, no brains, no brains.

---

[4] *ngoko* is a Matengo word for the things that chickens scratch the ground for and eat. They can be worms or grains or other things.

48

You took away my chicks, no brains
No brains, no brains, no brains

She approached another house.

"Please," she began, "have you, by any chance, seen Crow pass this way?"

"She went to the river to feed her chicks with *ngoko*," they told her.

Hawk went behind the house:

Mwakanakoungou malangu nzeilalei,
Malangu nzeilalei, nzeilalei, nzeilalei.
Mwakanakoungou malangu nzeilalei,
Malangu nzeilalei, nzeilalei, nzeilalei.
Mwakanitole banangu nzeilalei,
Banangu nzeilalei, nzeilalei, nzeilalei.

You, Crows, you have no brains,
No brains, no brains, no brains.
You, Crows, you have no brains,
No brains, no brains, no brains.
You took away my chicks, no brains,
No brains, no brains, no brains.

She moved on. She went and called Chameleon and Frog. She said:

"Divine for me; someone has run away with my chicks."

"Let's go," they said.

They went and sat on a rock. They said:

"Chameleon, you start."

"You start," Chameleon told Frog. So, Frog started:

Pein! Pein! Sei kilanga!
Pein! Pein! Sei kilanga!

Pein! Pein! It is a calamity!
Pein! Pein! It is a calamity!

Chameleon took over:

Katipu! Katipu! Katipu! Kihoumbi ngo!
Ngandanganda, masi swe!
Katipu! Katipu! Katipu! Kihoumbi ngo!
Ngandanganda, masi swe!

Katipu! Katipu! Katipu! Up swirls the dust!
Muddy! Muddy! Muddy! And water squirts
out!
Katipu! Katipu! Katipu! Up swirls the dust!
Muddy! Muddy! Muddy! And water squirts
out!

They saw the rock move and tumble away
mbilimbilimbili!

As the rock moved from its position, it exposed
Crow to sight; for she had been hiding underneath
the rock.

Hawk flared up:

"You escaped with my chicks, didn't you?"

"No," cried Crow. "I came to give them water to
drink. They had been crying with thirst."

"Eh?" exclaimed Hawk aggressively, and a fight
ensued between the two.

Crow got killed.

And that is the end of the tale.

Comments on
Hawk and Crow

This is a tale of crime and punishment. It is a very straightforward tale, told with remarkable economy of words.

Right from the beginning, Hawk appears to be more assertive than Crow. Hawk is the one who suggests or proposes things: "let's go lay eggs;" "Crow, stay with the chicks, I'm going to fish." Although Crow seems the more passive of the two, she soon proves herself different. As soon as Hawk has gone away, Crow runs away with all the chicks. We begin to realize that perhaps Crow's appearance of humility conceals an evil active heart.

There is no doubt that Crow is an evil character. She demonstrates this throughout the tale. First, she runs away with the chicks, taking advantage of Hawk's absence. Then, as she escapes with the chicks, she tells lies to the people who live in the homesteads through which she passes, saying that she is going down to the river to feed the chicks. Finally, when she is discovered by Frog and Chameleon, she tells the lie that she had come to give the chicks water to drink. Crow is killed in the end. In this way, evil is punished and innocence recompensed.

Our sympathies lie with Hawk as she moves from village to village in search of Crow and the chicks. What is curious about this tale is that somehow, as soon as Hawk saw that Crow and the chicks were missing, she knew that Crow had run away, not just that she was not home. In other words, Hawk knew that Crow had done some mischief. Even when people on the way told her that Crow had gone to the river, Hawk went behind their houses and sang her song, calling Crows half-wits. In this song she states that Crow has stolen her chicks. It seems that in the course of staying together with Crow, Hawk knew that Crow could not be trusted.

We find in this tale an even blend of dialogue and narrative; coupled with the brisk pace of the tale, which derives from its economy with words, it invests the tale with an unmistakable sense of both suspense and urgency.

In addition to this harmonious, even balance between dialogue and narrative, we see in this tale songs and incantations, all of which have very definite and important functions in the tale.

To begin with, there is Hawk's song. This song registers Hawk's view of Crow and her whole clan— that they are half-wits. In her song, Hawk justifies the revenge she is going to take upon Crow. By singing it again and again, Hawk helps to keep alive the fire of her vengeful spirit, which is nevertheless legitimate. In summary, then, this song expresses, rationalizes, and sustains Hawk's legitimate displeasure at what Crow has done. In actual story telling situations, this song intensifies the audience's sympathy with Hawk.

Then there are the songs and incantations of the diviners, Frog and Chameleon. These songs are part of the divination, and are a vehicle for the divination process. A diviner, like a magician, needs to use the appropriate words to bring about the desired results.

To start with, let us look at Frog's song. In the original Matengo, *"Pein! Pein! Sei kilanga!"* is sung by the narrator. *Pein* is an ideophone that reminds the audience of resounding noise such as that made by an axe cutting a dry and hard tree trunk or log. It is not clear from the tale whether Frog was hitting something to produce the sound *pein* while divining—and this seems most likely—or whether he simply sang the *pein*. The second possibility is rather unlikely. It is almost certain that Frog sang the phrase *sei kilanga*, since this phrase has a meaning. In translation, it means something like "Beware, calamity is coming!"

Chameleon's song embodies a number of meanings, some overt and others not so overt. *Katipu katipu* is an ideophone suggesting the action of beating dusty ground, especially stomping on it and producing clouds of dust. "*Kihoumbi ngo!*" clinches the meaning of this ideophone; for it means something like "And up swirls the dust!"

"*Nganda! Nganda!*" is an ideophone that suggests the process whereby things, especially wet soil, are transformed by vigorous activity into mud. "*Masi swee!*" is a phrase which means something like "And water squirts out!" The word "*swee!*" describes a sudden, forceful emission or ejaculation.

Frog's divination formula, then, could be translated as follows:

> *Pein! Pein!* It is a calamity!
> *Pein! Pein!* It is a calamity!

Chameleon's formula could be translated as follows:

> *Katipu! Katipu! Katipu!* Up swirls the dust!
> Muddy! Muddy! Muddy! And water squirts out!
> *Katipu! Katipu! Katipu!* Up swirls the dust!
> Muddy! Muddy! Muddy! And water squirts out!

Magic plays a key role in this tale. The discovery of runaway Crow and the chicks is effected by magical means, in the form of the divination performed by Frog and Chameleon. The words that accompany the action in this divination constitute the abracadabra that sends the rock tumbling away, exposing Crow and the chicks to view.

The deeds of Hawk and Crow provide a portrait of typical human actions; the tale is a mirror held up to a particular aspect of social life—crime and punishment. Here we see how an innocent person is wronged by an evil person and how, in the end, justice is done. We use the term poetic justice to describe this kind of outcome: when the guilty are punished and the innocent rewarded or vindicated.

This tale is a parable. It uses non-human characters to tell about human situations in such a way that we can draw lessons from their actions.

The Monster in the Rice Field

There was a man with five children. The children went to the rice field to watch over the rice. When they got to the field they went into the watch-hut.

Presently they saw a monster coming. The monster asked them:

"What have you children come to do here?"

"We came to watch over the rice," the children answered, and they began to sing:

> *Twa tuleindei mpounga, twa tuleindei mpounga;*
> *Twa tuleindei mpounga, twa tuleindei mpounga:*
> *Nanzwatu, twa tuleindei mpounga;*
> *Nanzwatu, twa tuleindei mpounga.*

> We are watching over the rice, we are
>   watching over the rice;
> We are watching over the rice, we are
>   watching over the rice;
> Nanzwatu, we are watching over the rice;
> Nanzwatu, we are watching over the rice.

The monster grabbed one of the children, and there remained four.

The four children went to their father and said:

"Our companion has been taken by a monster." The father said kindly:

"Just go, it is alright."

The children came to the field again. They went to sit in their usual place.

Presently they saw the monster coming again. It asked them:

"What did you come to do?"

"We came to watch over the rice," the children said, and started their song:

> Twa tuleindei mpounga, twa tuleindei mpounga;
> Twa tuleindei mpounga, twa tuleindei mpounga;
> Nanzwatu,twa tuleindei mpounga.

> We are watching over the rice, we are watching over the rice;
> We are watching over the rice, we are watching over the rice;
> Nanzwatu, we are watching over the rice.

The monster seized one of the children, and there remained three. The three went home and said:

"Our companion has been taken by a monster."

"Just go," they were told, gently.

When they got to the field, the children sat where they used to sit every day. The monster came again.

"What did you come here for?" it asked them.

"We came to watch over the rice," said the children, and they began to sing:

> Twa tuleindei mpounga, twa tuleindei mpounga;
> Twa tuleindei mpounga, twa tuleindei mpounga;
> Nanzwatu, twa tuleindei mpounga.

> We are watching over the rice, we are watching over the rice;
> We are watching over the rice, we are watching over the rice;
> Nanzwatu, we are watching over the rice.

The monster seized one of the children. There remained two.

The two children went home and said:

"Our companion has been taken by a monster."

"Just go," came the gentle reply.

The children came to the field again and sat at their usual place.

Presently, the monster came along. It asked them:

"What did you come to do?"

"We came to watch over the rice," said the children, and they began to sing:

> *Twa tuleindei mpounga, twa tuleindei mpounga;*
> *Twa tuleindei mpounga, twa tuleindei mpounga;*
> *Nanzwatu, twa tuleindei mpounga.*

> We are watching over the rice, we are
>   watching over the rice;
> We are watching over the rice, we are
>   watching over the rice;
> Nanzwatu, we are watching over the rice.

The monster took away one child, and now, four children were gone. There remained one child. The one child went home and said:

"Our companion has been taken by a monster."

"Just go," they said, calmly.

The child came to the field and sat at the same place. The same things happened.

> *Twa tuleindei mpounga, twa tuleindei mpounga;*
> *Twa tuleindei mpounga, twa tuleindei mpounga;*
> *Nanzwatu, twa tuleindei mpounga.*

> We are watching over the rice, we are
>   watching over the rice;

We are watching over the rice, we are
     watching over the rice;
Nanzwatu, we are watching over the rice.

All the five children got lost. The father came to
the field to keep watch.
The monster appeared. It asked:
"What have you come here for?"
"To watch over the rice," he said, and he started
the song:

Twa tuleindei, mpounga twa tuleindei mpounga;
Twa tuleindei mpounga, twa tuleindei mpounga;
Nanzwatu, twa tuleindei mpounga.

We are watching over the rice, we are
     watching over the rice;
We are watching over the rice, we are
     watching over the rice;
Nanzwatu, we are watching over the rice.

The monster seized the father, and there remained
the mother.
The mother, too, came to the field to keep watch.
She sat down. Then, she saw the monster coming. The
monster asked:
"What have you come to do here?"
"To watch over the rice," she said, and started to
sing:

Twa tuleindei mpounga, twa tuleindei mpounga;
Twa tulendei mpounga, twa tuleindei mpounga;
Nanzwatu, twa tuleindei mpounga.

We are watching over the rice, we are
     watching over the rice;

58

We are watching over the rice, we are
    watching over the rice;
Nanzwatu, we are watching over the rice.

The monster seized the mother.
And that is the end of the tale.

Comments on
The Monster in the Rice Field

Rice, which looms so large in this tale, is not a common staple in the Matengo highlands. It is mainly grown in the lowlands bordering on these highlands. How, then, is it that rice, rather than any other grain, occupies such a prominent place in this tale? Could it be that this tale did not originate in Matengo society but migrated there from elsewhere. This is very likely.

This is a tale about a peasant family in trouble. They have worked hard: tilling the land, planting the rice, and taking good care of it, but before they can harvest the rice, they have to deal with yet another problem—the various pests and animals that prey on the crop. In this tale, both adults and children work hard. The children are sent out to the rice field to keep watch, to ward off the birds and these other destructive creatures.

There is much realism in this tale; for example, Matengo children help out in farm work just as described in this tale. I remember the many days I spent with other children guarding our family wheat fields against birds. We would sing songs and make noises such as banging on empty tins, to chase away the birds. Because of the cold, we always made fires to warm ourselves.

There are, nevertheless, some unusual and enigmatic elements in the tale. How is it that these people take death so calmly? We see the children perishing, one after the other, but their father neither

60

gets depressed nor gives up. Again and again, with unbelievable calmness, he tells the remaining children to go back to the field. Why does this man take the death of his children so casually?

The children themselves do not seem to be afraid of the monster at all. When their father tells the remaining children to go back to the field, they do so, without the slightest hesitation. How realistic is this reaction of theirs? Finally, how is it that the woman, the mother of the children, is not herself shaken or heart-broken after the death of all her children and her husband? How do we explain that, having lost all her children and husband, this woman simply goes to the field, going the same way they went, to meet the same fate?

There is also a song in this tale. The first time the monster asks the children what they have come to do in the rice field, they answer that they have come to watch over the rice. Having said that, they start singing the song, which is, basically, a repetition of the answer. They mention in their song the name of Nanzwatu. Is Nanzwatu the name of the monster? We do not know, but this is very likely.

In their song, the children say *we* are watching over the rice. That is quite alright. But how is it that when the last child sings the song he still says *we* are watching over the rice, in stead of *I* am watching over the rice? How is it that their father sings exactly in the same way—*we* are watching over the rice? How is it that the mother, too, sings the song the same way? Why do all of them use the plural form, we, even when each of them is alone?

Furthermore, how is it that these people sing the same song? Did they practice it together at home before any of them went to the field? Or could it be that this is the song people normally sang while keeping watch over the rice? In other words, is this supposed to be a popular work song? If such is the case, if, in other words, this is supposed to be a stock song that people would normally sing while keeping watch in the rice fields, then it is possible that Nanzwatu is not the name of the monster in this tale. That, however, is only a possibility, since it is also possible that Nanzwatu is the name of the monster in this tale.

What is, or what could be, the point of this tale? Are these people blindly going to their deaths? As we have noted, these people are not even afraid of death. They go to their death calmly, deliberately. Why is this so? Is it because they take death as just a fact of life, on the same level as birth, illness, or old age, so that there is no fear in these people of a fact of life like death? Or is it that these people value their rice more than they value their own lives?

Before they are picked up by the monster, these people sing their soft song. The song does not comment on death, which is a central reality in the tale. The song is not a plea for life either, which would be most natural, when people are facing such a danger. It just states the nature of the work these people are doing: "we are watching over the rice." Considering that the monster in this tale is an agent or symbol of death, we can see that these people defy death while working. They work and defy death. In a very real sense, they work unto death.

This song, then, and the tale itself, express the toil and suffering of the peasants in their struggle against nature. The song and the tale pay tribute to the heroism of the peasants. As we can see, the peasants in this tale, whether young or old, male or female, are heroic in the best sense of the word.

Let us turn, now, to the monster. Is the monster in this tale evil or just hungry? Does this monster symbolize anything in particular? Does it, for example, represent Fate? Does it, as I have suggested, represent Death? If this is the case, the tale is intended to instruct us that we must engage in productive work and not be discouraged by any setbacks. We must have determination even if it costs us our lives. This seems to be one of the messages of the tale.

The children are another subject. They are very obedient and innocent. Because of this, their death is shocking. They do not deserve to die. In fact, all the people in this tale do not deserve their deaths. They are just hard-working peasants who have done no wrong. Is the tale suggesting that life is absurd? If innocent people can come to such a terrible end, what is the meaning of life?

The woman in this tale deserves some comment. She does not fit the conventional stereotype of a woman as weak and passive. She is extremely courageous, with nerves of steel. Having lost her children and her husband, she is not heart-broken. She goes out to the field to face the same fate that has met her children and her husband. As if to highlight the unusual courage of this woman, the tale presents her very strategically—she is the one who is made to witness and suffer the deaths of all the others, and having undergone this extraordinary ordeal, she emerges as strong as ever and boldly goes to the field. It is chiefly by making her the last person to go to the field that the tale manages to present the courage of this woman in such bold relief.

Is the depiction of the woman believable or truthful? This is, again, a question of realism, of the relationship of the tale to social reality. Does this woman typify the Matengo woman, past or present?

This may not be the proper way to frame the question. We might ask, first, whether there is or has ever been the typical Matengo woman. If we agree that such a woman exists or has existed, the next question would be whether the nature of the typical Matengo woman has remained the same throughout the ages. Even if, for the sake of argument, we were to say that the typical modern Matengo woman is not as courageous as the one we see in this tale, is it not possible that the typical Matengo woman of some point in the past was a courageous woman such as we see in this tale? I think it is most likely.

Let us remember that the past in Matengo history has been one of great uncertainty due to various problems. People had to migrate from place to place, braving hostile natural forces and hostile people. Wars and raids have at certain times enforced great hardships on the Matengo. Obviously, to survive all these hardships required courage in both men and women. There is not the slightest doubt that the Matengo woman of the past must have been a person seasoned and tempered in hardships. The courage of the woman in this tale could, therefore, be seen as a realistic portrayal in the context of the past, at least. Since the tale comes to us from the past, we may not have much reason to dispute this.

We must remember that the weakness and passivity of women is not innate or God-given, but historically and socially conditioned. A historical situation in which both men and women are thrown into the center of socio-economic struggles brings out the supreme courage latent in both men and women. The weakness of women and their passivity have been created and continue to be maintained by their being banished from the struggles of life, by their being denied opportunities to demonstrate and cultivate their latent qualities. Instead of being given all the opportunities that men get, women have been locked up in the kitchen, with the result, to quote Lenin, that the woman "continues to be a *domestic slave*, because *petty housework* crushes, strangles, stultifies and degrades her, chains her to the kitchen and the nursery, and she wastes her labour on barbarously unproductive, petty, nerve-racking, stultifying and crushing drudgery."[5]

The plot of this tale is very simple and very easy to remember mainly because it follows a repetitive pattern. What happens is essentially the same incident—people going to the field and being seized by the monster. This is repeated many times. In this tale, we find, as we normally do in folktales, a harmonious blend of narrative, dialogue, and song. The tale represents the human ability to manipulate various forms of verbal art and synthesize them in a unified work or art.

From all that I have said about this tale, it would appear that behind the seeming simplicity and "pointlessness" of this tale lies a profound vision of and penetrating commentary on social life.

---

[5] V.I. Lenin, "A Great Beginning," *The Lenin Anthology*, selected and edited by Robert C. Tucker (New York: W.W. Norton & Company, Inc. 1975), p. 484.

An Uncle
and His Nephew

There was once a man, and he married a woman. After he had married her, he said to her:

"My wife, I don't like you to give birth to female babies. I want only male babies."

After some time, naturally, the wife conceived, She gave birth to a female baby! The man took the baby and killed it.

Time passed and the woman conceived again. She gave birth to another female baby, and the man killed it. The woman asked:

"Why is it that you kill the babies I give birth to? If it is God's will that we should have female children, how can we prevent it?"

The man refused to listen to these words, and he insisted that he did not like female children and that he would kill them as soon as they were born.

They stayed for some time, and the wife became pregnant again. In due course, a female baby was born, and the man killed it.

This went on until six babies had been born and killed. Then the woman conceived again. At last, she gave birth to a male baby.

The child grew well and became a youth. The woman conceived again and gave birth to a female baby. The man said:

"I must kill this baby!"

The youth said:

"You're not going to kill this baby! I need a sister. I don't like to live alone in this house."

When the man heard this, he could not believe his ears, and he became very angry.

"Get out of my house," he roared. "Disappear, you and your sister! I have said I want only male children here."

The two children left and went away, not knowing where they were going. They just went on and on, into the unknown. They walked and walked and walked.

At last, they met a bird on the way. The bird asked them:

"Where are you going?"

"We don't know where we are going," the children answered. "Our father has thrown us out of his house. He wanted to kill this sister of mine, and I told him that I was not going to allow that to happen. He had killed many sisters of mine before, and he was going to kill this one too."

The bird was moved with compassion, and it said to the boy:

"Get onto my wing."

And to the girl it said:

"And you, too, get onto my other wing."

When the two children had climbed onto the bird's wings, the bird flew away with them. It carried them very, very far away, until they reached a very big town.

When it had set them down, the bird showed them the whole town. It gave them the keys of all the houses in that town and told them:

"Feel free to go wherever you like in this town, and to use whatever you want to use. You will be the rulers of this place."

The bird, then, showed the children the door of one of the houses and said:

"Don't ever open this door here. Leave it alone!"

After it had told them these words, the bird flew away and left them there.

The two children started living in that town, and, every day, the brother used to go down to the river to catch fish, which they cooked and ate.

Now it happened that whenever the brother was down at the river fishing, the sister, back home, used to search through the bundles of keys, looking for the key of the forbidden house.

One day, she found that key. She opened the forbidden door, and suddenly a huge snake came out of the house, grabbed her and swept her inside, saying:

"You're now going to be my wife!"

That very instant, the huge snake made the poor girl pregnant, and immediately she gave birth to a baby! At once the baby grew up, got out of the house, and made for the river, calling:

"Uncle! Uncle! Uncle!"

The brother down at the river heard the voice and was greatly puzzled. He asked himself:

"Who can be calling me in that way? Aren't there only two of us in this town—my sister and I?"

The boy got closer and closer, calling all the while:

"Uncle! Uncle! Uncle!"

When the boy reached his uncle, he declared:

"I'm your nephew. You remember that when the bird brought you to this town, it forbade you to enter one of the houses. Your sister has opened and entered it, and, as a result, I have been born. I'm your nephew."

The uncle was still puzzled, and the boy continued:

"My advice to you is this: don't go back to the town. There is a huge snake there, who is my father. The moment he sees you, he will kill you. However, I know what we can do to avoid all this. When we get home, I will hide you in a room. I will cook the fish you have caught and bring them to you in that room."

The two of them left the river and began going home. The uncle was full of fear about what might happen.

When they came home, the nephew hid his uncle in a room and went to cook the fish. His father, the snake, saw him and asked:

"You, where did you get those fish?"

The son answered:

"I got them from my uncle down at the river."

"I don't want anybody else around here," said the snake. "I know only three persons here—your mother, you, and myself. Do you hear?"

The son said that his uncle must be allowed to live there with them.

The snake did not say anything else, and the uncle continued living there. And he continued going down to the river every day to catch fish.

But the snake was not happy to see the man around, and it kept thinking of ways and means to destroy him.

One day, the man caught two fish. The snake managed, somehow, to get hold of them. It cut open one of them and spit poison into it, knowing that its own son would serve the fish to his uncle.

When the son had cooked the fish, he sent them in to his uncle, but he deliberately gave him the fish that was not poisoned. He himself ate the poisoned fish, for he knew that snake poison could not harm him, because he had snake's blood in his veins.

Now, the snake was confident that the man would die immediately, after eating the poisoned fish. But it was amazed that things did not turn out as it had expected; for it saw the man continue living in perfect health!

One day, the snake decided to use other means to kill the man. It resolved to follow him to the river where he was fishing, intending to swallow him up.

The snake's son sensed that his father had an evil scheme in mind. He left immediately and went down to the river, carrying six pangas. He came to the river before his father, the snake, arrived.

Soon afterwards, however, a violent wind arose, brought about by the coming snake. The nephew told his uncle, who was visibly shaking with fear:

"Uncle, don't worry; I'll deal with the situation."

In spite of these assurances, the uncle was very much afraid, and the boy kept reassuring him.

Then, suddenly, the nephew became alert and stood firm. Just then, with the wind blowing very violently, one of the snake's six heads appeared, with forked tongue and flaming eyes. The young man hurled his panga at the snake's head. The panga chopped off the head and broke up.

The second head appeared, as horrifying as the first. The young man flung another panga at it, chopped it off, and the panga broke up. The third head appeared. The young man hurled another panga at it, chopped it off, and the panga broke up. The same thing happened when the fourth and fifth heads appeared.

With only one head remaining, the snake, angry, and agonized, spoke out:

"So, you want to kill me?"

The son answered:

"I must kill you. I want to stay with only my uncle and my mother."

The snake made a last, desperate bid to strike, but the young man let go his sixth panga. It chopped off the snake's head and broke up. The snake died, bleeding profusely. Its blood flowed into the river and flooded it.

When all this was over, the uncle said:

"I must go back and kill my sister. I don't need her, and I don't like to have anything to do with her, after all she has done—bringing me to the brink of death."

When they got home, the uncle summoned his sister:

"You, what did the bird tell us about the house? Why did you open it? You wanted me to die, didn't you? I'm killing you right here and now."

He killed her there and then.

From that day onwards, the uncle and the nephew lived alone in that town. They used to go down to the river everyday to catch fish for food.

One day, the uncle said:

"How long are we going to live alone without wives?"

The nephew replied:

"That is an important question. My opinion is that you, rather than I, should get yourself a wife."

The uncle objected, saying:

"I think *you* should marry, because you managed to kill that huge snake, your father. You have proved yourself a real man, compared to me."

The nephew said:

"It's you who should marry, because you are older than me."

"That can't be," said the uncle. "*You* must marry; for you did kill your father, who would have killed me. I would be dead now, if it had not been for you. I owe my life to you!"

The nephew answered:

"If we cannot agree on this point, we can settle it otherwise. Let us fight; whoever is thrown down will have to marry.

The uncle agreed with this idea, but he added:

"I know, even though, that you'll easily beat me; for you managed to kill your father, the snake. And what am I, compared to that huge snake?"

"Don't mind that," the nephew said. "Let's just fight. My idea is this: as we fight, the one who gets too tired to continue fighting will be the one to marry."

With this, the matter was settled, and they began to fight. They fought very furiously, like sworn enemies, and if you had seen them, you wouldn't have believed that they were relatives. Eventually, the uncle became very tired, and it was clear that he could not continue with the fight. The nephew said:

"It doesn't matter. Let us move from this place. We shall go to a place where we can get plenty of women."

By then they had already forgotten all about their fight, and they had become friendly to each other again. You would not have believed that they were the very ones who had fought so savagely only a moment before! Although the uncle had been bruised in the fight, his nephew had already applied some saliva on the bruises, and they had now healed. The two of them resolved to go away from that place, saying:

"Let's go on and on, no matter where. We shall certainly reach a land where women are plentiful."

So, they set out. They walked; they walked, and they walked. At last, they reached a town. They were greatly amazed by what they saw in that town.

The people of that town never dared to draw water from their well without first throwing someone into the well! There was a huge, eleven-headed snake living in that well, which demanded that a human sacrifice be made to it before anyone could draw water from that well. As a result of this, the people of that town lived in great misery.

Now it happened that when the uncle and his nephew were entering that town, the people of the town were on their way to the well, carrying the queen with them. They were going to sacrifice her to the snake in the well, in order to get water.

When the nephew saw this, he interrupted the procession, declaring:

"Don't throw her into the well! Let her free. Bring your pots and buckets here. I'll draw water for you, as much as you want. Damn the snake! It can't do anything to me!"

The people brought him their pots and buckets to see what he would do. Immediately the young man got into the well, and plunged himself into the task of drawing water for the people, not caring a jot for the snake that had emerged from the well and was trying to get him.

To everybody's amazement, the huge snake was powerless to harm him in any way. All it could do was lick him here and there. And while he was busily engaged in drawing the water, the young man talked contemptuously about the snake. He said:

"Ah! How can people fear this mean and worthless creature!"

And turning to the people he said:

"Bring your pots here. I'll draw water for you all, and let's see what this worthless snake will do! I normally have no time to waste on things like this snake here. I just ignore them!"

When the young man had given everybody the water they needed, he asked them:

"Tell me, if I do away with this snake, what will you give me?"

The people answered unanimously:

"If you eliminate this abominable creature for us, we'll make you our king."

"Are you serious?" the young man asked them.

"We mean what we say," they answered.

"Now," said the young man, "watch how I silence this mean creature!"

And with these words, he descended into the well with eleven pangas. He chopped the huge snake to pieces with incredible ease and finished it off.

When the people saw what the young man had done, they rejoiced very much and heaped many presents on him. And, as they had promised, they made him king of that town. From that day onwards, everybody lived in great happiness.

One day, the king thought:

"My uncle is here with me. How long shall I let him live without an important post? It were best I found him a post somewhere."

So, the king set out with his uncle and they came to one town. The king gave him a job there. The uncle worked diligently at his job and he got promotion after promotion until, eventually, he became king of that town.

Comments on
An Uncle and his Nephew

This tale is, by and large, a study in contrasts. The irrationality of the husband who demands male babies is contrasted with the rationality of his wife, who asks: "If it is God's will that we should have female babies, how can we prevent it?" The cruelty of the father, who rejects his own children, is contrasted with the kindness of the mother, who defends them. This cruelty is contrasted also with the kindness of the bird, which, though a complete stranger to the children, helps them out of their predicament.

The interplay of contrasts continues even after the setting of the tale has shifted to the distant town. Here, freedom and constraint are among the conflicting forces. The children are free to open all doors, but are prohibited to open one. They are free to roam the town, but the snake is confined to his room.

The misguided curiosity and disobedience of the girl are contrasted with the principled behaviour and obedience of her brother. The snake is inhospitable to the uncle, while the nephew is hospitable towards him, going to the extent of ensuring that he is not harmed, whether by poisoning or other means.

There is also a contrast between the uncle and his nephew. The uncle is weak and not quite brave, while the nephew is confident and very strong, both mentally and physically.

The pattern of contrasts continues to manifest itself in the third stage of the tale, after the uncle and his nephew have arrived in the town that is tormented by the snake in the well. Here, the suffering of the town before the arrival of the two young men is contrasted with the happiness that comes after the young men have arrived and taught the snake a lesson.

The tale achieves a good balance between good and evil, weakness and strength, despair and hope, failure and success. As a result, the tale projects a rather optimistic view of life: evil or other negative forces cannot triumph forever.

This message is brought home at various stages in the tale. At the very beginning, we see how the man's wicked scheme to kill his last daughter is thwarted by a mere boy, his own son. Later, the father snake that seeks to kill the uncle is killed by its own son. Towards the end of the tale, the snake that torments the town is, similarly, killed by the brave nephew, enabling the townsfolk to live happily thereafter.

The tale deals extensively with the theme of killing; it deals with infanticide, parricide, and filicide. All of this arises in the context of the struggle between fathers and sons or characters we might consider father figures and son figures. The theory of psychoanalysis would call this an Oedipal struggle.

The man at the beginning of the tale has a struggle with his son, although neither of them gets killed. This man has an evil heart, like a monster. The dragon, the monster, and the snake are father figures; they have their own life-and-death struggles with their sons or characters we can consider son figures. In this they resemble the man at the beginning of the tale, who as I have noted, has the heart of a monster. The dragon, the monster, and the snake are mirror images of that man.

The theme of conflict predominates in this tale. At the beginning of the tale, we see the husband pitted against his wife. The wife, on her part, is pitted against fate—the impersonal and inscrutable fate which decides whether she should have female or male babies. Then we see the son pitted against the father, a confrontation resulting in the expulsion of the son and his sister from their father's house. This conflict between father and son is common in folklore, and it can be discussed as a manifestation of the Oedipus complex.

Having been expelled, the two children are condemned to wander in the wilderness, pitted against fate. Later, the nephew takes a stand against the snake, his own father. Towards the end of the tale, the town is pitted against the big snake in the well.

As it begins, the tale touches on the theme of father right, that is, the rights fathers tend to have over the children in most cultures. Children belong to the father, and the father has ultimate authority over them. The tale suggests the way in which this right can be abused, since the father uses it to kill the children he does not like.

The tale shows how this right can have dire consequences for the mother as well, who has no comparable rights, but bears, instead, the burden of seeing her children being killed. We see that the man, the head of the family, holds absolute power over the life of his children. The wife can only ask "How is it that you kill the babies I give birth to? If it is God's will that we should have female babies, how can we prevent it?"

The woman seems to be criticizing the injustice inherent in the system of male domination and the injustice in the unequal estimation and treatment of sons and daughters. The woman seems to be championing human equality, the equality of the sexes, to be specific, by her statement that children are willed by God, whether they are male or female.

Matengo society is male dominated. In that context, the ideas propagated by the woman in this tale are subversive. We are forced to ask ourselves how such ideas emerged, persisted, and continue to circulate in the society. The presence of such ideas in a male dominated society reminds us that the function of folklore is not simply or always to reflect or propagate the values of a society. Folklore can also question or challenge those values.

This tale not only points out that the ideology and practice of male domination is unjust; it also points out that this ideology can produce negative or destructive consequences, as is exemplified by the killing of the baby girls in this tale.

It is not easy to understand, let alone justify, this man's insistence that he wants only male babies. If, however, we decide to rely on facts other than those given in the tale, we could say that perhaps the man's seemingly irrational demand stems from the issue of heirs, the question of perpetuating one's name, which is central in societies at a certain stage of development.

In societies where inheritance follows the male line, a man desires sons. In such societies, a woman is more respected by her husband and by the rest of society if she bears at least one son. In Matengo society, although daughters are desirable because they bring cows and goats when they get married, couples still desire sons. Paradoxically, though sons are a great burden when the time comes for them to be provided with bride wealth, a man does not complain if he happens to have only sons and no daughters. The wife, though, will complain, because there is no one to help her with her household chores.

The wife in this tale is very tolerant. Though she goes through the ordeal of her husband killing her children, she is very restrained. Only much later does she speak out; when she does, she is still very restrained and sensible. Such is the image we get of this woman.

But does the tale attempt to generalize about women? Does it project a view of women as all good? Not at all. There is the girl in this tale who, unable to contain her curiosity, opens the forbidden door. This one is depicted as irresponsible and disobedient.

In the same way, this tale does not present all men as being all irrational, like the one who kills his children. There is the boy, this man's son, who is reasonable and courageous. He opposes his irrational father, and he follows the bird's instructions carefully.

This tale depicts men and women with much realism and even-handedness. It does not stereotype them. Although the girl caused much harm by her disobedience, this tale does not project the idea that women are the source of evil. The tale depicts men as being capable of irresponsible behaviour and causing evil things to happen.

The fantastic element is noticeable in this tale. It is manifested in the relationship between human beings and various animals or animal-like creatures. A girl is forcibly married to a snake, and the product of this marriage is a child of extraordinary abilities.

This child resembles epic heroes in many ways: the strange circumstances surrounding his birth, his superhuman physical and mental abilities, and his combat with the deadly enemy. We see that no adversary can defeat him. He also has the ability to read the thoughts of others and foresee things to come. He even knows, without being told, things which happened before he was born.

The Tale of
Two Women

There were once two women. Each of them gave birth to a baby.

After they had borne their babies, one of them said to the other:

"Let's pound our babies in a mortar."

The second woman agreed. The first woman was planning to make the other woman pound her baby, but she was not planning to pound her own. She told the other woman:

"We shall not pound our babies together. You will go one way, and I will go another way."

And so they separated, each of them going to pound her baby out of sight of the other.

Now, the first woman took some maize particles and pounded them instead of her baby.

The second woman went and pounded her baby. When she saw the first woman sifting what she had pounded, she remarked:

"So, you've already finished pounding yours?"

The first woman answered with a sneer:

"Do you think I was pounding my baby? I was just pounding some maize particles."

The second woman spoke out, distressed:

"But I have pounded my baby! Why did you deceive me so?"

"That's your own problem," answered the first woman arrogantly. "Who told you to believe me?" she added.

The second woman did not like to quarrel; she simply said:

"You have deceived me, but it doesn't matter. I'm going to my aunt. She'll help me in this, I'm sure."

So, the second woman set out, on the journey to her aunt. She walked and walked and walked. Then, she met someone on the way, whose body was covered all over with wounds and jiggers. The person asked her calmly:

"Where are you going?"

"I'm going to my aunt," said the woman, "to seek her help." I had a baby, and some other woman has tricked me into pounding it in a mortar."

"Is it so?" asked the person.

"It is so," the woman said.

Then, the person asked:

"Will you please take out my jiggers for me?"

The woman immediately sat down and started taking out the jiggers.

When she had taken out all the jiggers the person asked her:

"Will you please lick my wounds?"

The woman promptly obeyed and set about licking the wounds. When she had licked all the wounds, she continued on her way.

After she had walked for a long time, she met another person with wounds all over the body. The person asked:

"Where are you going?"

And the woman said:

"I'm going to my aunt to look for babies. I had a baby and some other woman has tricked me into pounding it in a mortar."

"Really?" exclaimed that person.

"It is so," answered the woman.

The person said:

"Will you lick my wounds before you go?"

The woman started to lick those wounds. When she had licked them all and was about to leave, the person told her:

"When you reach your aunt's home, do not go near the house, but stay some way off. You'll hear a cock crow. Now go, but remember my words."

The woman thanked that person and went on her way. When she got near her aunt's home, she stopped some distance from the house, as she had been instructed.

Then, a cock crowed:

"Ngou-ka-lei-kyee! Ageni kunduue!" (Cock-a-doodle doo! There's a guest near the house!).

Those who were in the house said:

"Listen, listen to the crowing of the cock."

They listened.

The cock crowed again:

"Ngou-ka-lei-kyee! Ageni kunduue!" (Cock-a-doodle doo! There is a guest near the house!).

And the people said to one another:

"The cock says there's a guest near the house. Will someone go and see?"

The aunt went out promptly, and soon she announced that indeed there was a guest outside. So, she welcomed her niece into the house.

After they had exchanged greetings, the aunt asked:

"My daughter, what is it that has brought you here?"

The woman then told her tale. She said:

"The woman I live with tricked me by saying that we should pound our babies in a mortar, and that each of us should go out sight of the other for this purpose. Now, while I pounded my baby, I did not know that she was not pounding hers."

All the people pitied that woman, and her aunt said:

"Don't worry. You will get other babies. Wait until evening, when we shall send you to one of the houses here, which has no door. When you are there, you'll have to bear many things. If a lion comes along to terrify you don't show any sign of fear and don't cry out. Lizards will come along and run all over you, but stay still. Remember that if you do not follow these instructions you won't get any babies. After all these trials, you'll hear a noise: *"Mbo-mbo-mbo-mbombombombo!"* When you hear this noise, hold your hand up in readiness to catch what will drop down. When you hear the noise: *"Ngengele-le-le-le!"* catch what drops down, for that will be the baby."

The woman promised to follow their words.

So, when evening came, they sent the woman to that house. She stayed there for some time and then the lion appeared. It roared and roared, but the woman kept calm.

"Rrr-rrr-rrr-rrr-mmmm!" roared the lion, in vain.

The lion vanished and lizards flooded the room. They ran all over the woman's body. The woman did not blink an eye. Hyenas came into the room and made terrible noises; then many other animals came too, but the woman remained calm. After all this, the room became quiet.

It was then that the woman heard the first sound: *"Mbo-mbo-mbo-mbombombombo!"*

She lifted her hands, ready to catch what would drop down.

Then, *"ngengelelelelele!"* and she caught the baby, a most beautiful baby, like an Indian baby.

As it was still night, the woman remained in that room. Soon the animals came again to terrify her; the lion came, the lizards, the hyenas and all the other animals. But the woman did not show any fear. Then it became calm again.

The sound came:

"Mbo-mbo-mbo-mbo-mbombombombo!"

The woman lifted her hands.

"Ngengelelelele!"

And the woman caught a second baby, as beautiful as the first. This was a girl.

Now it was morning, and the woman came out of that room and went into her aunt's house.

"Aunt!" she called out with joy. "I got two very beautiful babies.!"

"You see?" the aunt exclaimed happily. "Didn't we tell you to remain calm in the face of all those animals? Now see what you've got!"

The aunt took the babies in her arms.

"Now," she said, "you cannot go back home today. You must sleep here and tomorrow you can go."

The woman spent the night with her aunt and left the following morning.

She traveled for a long, long time until she reached the person with wounds.

That person said:

"Have you got the babies?"

"Indeed I have!" replied the woman.

The person said:

"You see?" Didn't I tell you that when you got to your aunt's home you should stay away from the house until you were called in? Now lick my wounds again."

The woman licked the wounds and then continued her journey. When she had walked for a long time, she met the second person with wounds. The woman licked that person's wounds and continued on her journey.

At last, she came home. The other woman saw her and when she saw the babies she found that they were very beautiful. And her own child looked dirty and unkempt. She said:

"How lucky you are to have such beautiful babies! I also must pound my child, and then I'll go and get beautiful babies like yours."

Immediately, that woman put her child in a mortar and pounded it. When she finished pounding it she brought a sieve and sifted the flour. And this flour she carried with her to her aunt. She set out on her journey without delay.

She walked and walked and walked. Then she met the person covered with wounds. The person asked:

"Where are you traveling to?"

She answered:

"I'm going to my aunt to get babies."

"Will you please lick my wounds?" the person inquired.

The woman burst into laughter.

"Hee-hee-hee-hee! You must be mad." she exclaimed with contempt. "I should lick your wounds! Why don't you lick them yourself?"

The person said:

"Alright, continue with your journey."

The woman left and went on her way. She walked for a long time, and then she met another person on the way, covered with wounds, like the first.

"Where are you going?" the person asked.

"I'm going to my aunt to get babies."

"Will you please lick my wounds?" asked the person.

The woman laughed with contempt:

"Hee-hee-heee! You must have lost your head! How dare you ask me to lick your wounds! So, you've been sitting here all this time fancying that I would come along and lick them. Sit there and wait; some fool might come around and lick your wounds, but not me. You can lick then yourself, for all I care."

With these words, the woman left and went on her way. The person with wounds did not tell her what to do on arriving at her aunt's home.

At last, the woman came to her destination and she made straight for the house.

"May I come in?" she called out as she came to the door.

They welcomed her in, and when she had been seated and the greetings had been exchanged she said:

"I've come looking for babies."

"You're looking for babies?" the people there asked her.

"Yes."

The aunt talked to her about what lay in store for her.

You know," she began, "we have certain customs here which all who come looking for babies have to follow. You'll have to go an spend the night in that house over there, which has no door. Lions will come to terrify you and leopards will come also, and hyenas and other animals.

"Your task is to remain calm and not to show the slightest fear. Do not stir and do not make any noise. After all this, you'll hear a sound: *"Mbo-mbo-mbo-mbombombombo*. When you hear this, raise your hands and be ready to catch what will come down. Another sound will follow: *'Ngengelelele!'*

"When you hear this, catch what falls down."

The woman promised to do as she had been instructed. So, when evening came, they escorted her to that house.

Night came. A lion appeared and roared with a horrible voice:

"*Rrrrrrmmmmmmmrrrrrmmmmm*"

The woman screamed and howled at the top of her voice. She screamed and howled when the leopards came and when the hyenas came. And when the lizards ran all over her body, she screamed and screamed.

After all this, the first sound came: "*Mbo-mbo-mbo-mbombombombo.!* The woman lifted her hands.

Another sound came: "*Ngengelelelele!*" The woman caught what was falling.

What a strange baby she caught! A half baby, with one leg, half a stomach, half a trunk, half a neck, half a mouth, half a face, half a head! The woman placed the baby beside her. After some time the animals appeared again and made as much havoc as before. The woman screamed and howled as loud as she could.

After the animals had gone, the sound came: "*Mbo-mbo-mbo-mbombombombo!* The woman lifted her hands.

Then came the other sound: "*Ngengelelelele!*"

The woman caught what was falling. A male baby! A half baby, like the first!

When it was morning, the woman got out of the house and went in to her aunt's house. And she told her aunt:

"I've got the babies."

Her voice indicated that she was not quite happy. The aunt said:

"How, now, what kind of babies have you got? Half babies! You screamed and howled, didn't you! We heard you!"

The woman replied:

"I was threatened by the lions and other beasts, and I feared for my life. I was only asking for help."

"Now," said the aunt, "what is this that you have done? You have ruined everything. Your colleague came and she heeded our words and did not make any noise when she encountered the animals. Now you'll stay here for the night, You can't make the journey home today; you'll go tomorrow."

The woman said she was not in favour of staying until the following day. She said she would like to start the journey home on that very day.

So, she said good bye and, taking her babies, she set out on the homeward journey.

She walked and walked and walked. Then she met the person with wounds. The person asked:

"How, now, have you got the babies?"

"Why, yes," answered the woman curtly, without even stopping, and she proceeded on her journey.

When she had gone for a very long time, she met the other person with wounds. The person asked:

"How, now, have you got the babies?"

"Why, yes," answered the woman.

"Let's see them," said the person. "What! Half babies! See? We told you: 'Lick our wounds,' and you just laughed us off."

The woman laughed with scorn even then:

"Hee-hee-hee! You're cranks if you think I'm the kind of person to lick your wounds!"

With these words, the woman went on her way.

When she came home, she saw the babies of the other woman. They had now grown and had reached walking age. They were very beautiful indeed.

Now, every day when she went to the fields she asked the other woman to allow her children to come along with her so that they could look after her babies while she was working. The other woman was always very willing to allow her children to go to the fields. Now the mother of the half babies took advantage of this, and one day she poisoned the beautiful children, and they died.

And that is the end of the tale.

Comments on
The Tale
of Two Women

We are not told, in this tale, if the two women are just neighbours or co-wives. Indeed, we do not know whether they are married at all, which would be the normal situation in Matengo culture.

Whatever their relationship, the two women seem to be on good terms as the tale begins. When the first woman suggest the idea of pounding the babies, the other one readily agrees. The way the tale is told, we are not supposed to raise questions about whether the idea of pounding babies is acceptable or not.

This equilibrium is, nevertheless, soon disturbed. We discover that it is a malicious scheme that impels the first woman to suggest the idea of pounding the babies, that she does not herself intend to pound her own baby, but only wants to ruin the other woman. At this point, the tale begins to reveal the first woman as evil.

From here onwards, the evil character of this woman continues to unfold. When the other woman expresses her sorrow at having been made to pound her baby, this woman laughs her off with a sneer. When she sees that the other woman has obtained beautiful babies, she boils over with envy and hastily decides to undertake the trip to her aunt to get babies of her own.

Now, when a Matengo woman goes on a formal visit, she prepares some flour to carry to the relative she is visiting. She carries it in a *lijamanda*, a kind of big basket with a lid. The woman in this tale takes flour to her aunt, which is in line with the customs. Nevertheless, the kind of flour she is taking is revolting; it is a grave insult to the custom itself. This reinforces the negative image of this woman.

This woman has neither respect nor kindness; this is clear from the way she ignores and insults the two wound-ridden persons she meets on the way. As she arrives at her aunt's home, she misbehaves by declaring the object of her visit as soon as the greetings are over. Such haste on the part of a *lijamanda* carrying guest is totally unbecoming.

A specific code of conduct goes with the *lijamanda*. When a guest carrying a *lijamanda* is spotted coming, the hostess goes out to meet her. She must, usually without any greetings being exchanged, get the *lijamanda* from the guest and carry it herself as she leads the way home. When they get home, the hostess must go and put the *lijamanda* in the house first. Then she sees to it that a stool is brought for the guest to sit on, and only after guest and hostess are comfortably seated do they greet each other and start conversing.

This woman has other flaws. She violates the instructions to keep calm during the night. On the following day, she leaves, practically in a hurry, which is totally unbecoming. On the way home, she insults the two destitutes, and she offers pert answers to their queries. When she comes home and sees the children of the other woman, her envy intensifies. Ultimately, she hatches and carries out her plot to kill these children.

This tale is told in such a way that both the narrator and the audience see the second woman as the complete opposite of the first. She is wholly good. This image comes about from what this woman does, says, and undergoes. She is made to suffer the death of her first child by the evil schemes of the first woman. Still, she does not take revenge. She is kind and humble, going to the extent of licking the wounds of the two destitutes on the way. Obedient and courageous, she follows all the instructions of her aunt.

This woman's trust in people knows no bounds. She accepts the idea of pounding babies, trusting that the other woman would pound hers. Towards the end of the tale, she readily allows the other woman to take her children to the field, believing that the other woman wants them as baby sitters.

Yet, upon closer scrutiny, one may want to ask whether the second woman is such a good person as the tale makes her. One might argue that this woman is also bad, for she agreed to the idea of pounding babies, and she pounded hers.

It is strange that she is not punished for this; her aunt does not even reprimand her. Although the aunt knows that this woman has pounded her baby, which is the same as saying that this woman is not a good mother, she gives her other babies. Is the aunt sensible? Think about this.

One of the central aspects of this tale is the test theme or motif. The two women are tested in various ways. The suggestion that the first woman puts forward, that they should pound their babies, is a test for the second woman. She could have said no, but she said yes. She got some punishment for this violation of the ideal of motherhood; she lost her child.

Each of these women is tested, and by means of the test motif or theme, the tale reveals the character of each woman.

The two women in this tale are the main characters. There are secondary characters as well: the aunt, the anonymous members of her household, the two destitutes on the way, and the children.

The aunt is a helper. She has the power and the will to help the two women to get babies. The only help she can render them, nevertheless, is to instruct them what to do; everything else depends on their own efforts.

The aunt is impartial; she accords each woman the same treatment, issuing to each the same instructions. The one who obeys the instructions succeeds in her quest; the one who ignores them fails. It is up to the individual to make the choices in life which eventually lead to success or failure. The aunt is not to blame for whatever happens. She has no pity either, for the woman who fails as a result of her own fault, but she congratulates the one who, having followed her instructions, succeeds.

The destitutes are also helpers. They also function as vehicles for the test motif in this tale. They are there to test the humility and kindness of the two women. The licking of wounds is a severe test, and we see why one woman fails it. The two destitutes are endowed with the power to aid the woman who fulfills their request to lick the wounds. In this way, the two destitutes embody both weakness and strength. Physically they are weak and helpless, but they have this supernatural ability to aid the women in their quest for babies. What I call their supernatural ability is their understanding of what lies ahead in the journey undertaken by the women.

The various creatures which come in the night are also vehicles of the test motif. They are quite mysterious; we don't know who actually controls them, telling them to come or go. Could it be that the aunt is a witch, who controls these creatures? Think about this.

The tale centers around the theme of motherhood, its responsibilities, joys, and anxieties. Motherhood implies children, and the tale deals with the theme of babies at length: infanticide, loss of babies, obtaining babies, normal babies, and deformed babies.

An interesting side of this tale is the way it avoids mentioning the natural way of obtaining children, through sex. There are no fathers here, and the tale resembles those tales of miraculous birth which go very far back in time. Jesus belongs in this category; he was born without a human father. The absence of the father, the denial of the role of the father, is a significant aspect of this tale.

The babies in this tale are passive characters, victims of forces beyond their control. They do not choose to be pounded nor do they choose to be poisoned. They do not choose to be born beautiful or ugly. Victims of the vagaries of fate or the folly of their parents, they suffer for things they had no hand in bringing about.

The progression of the incidents that make up this tale is a sequence of contradictions. This is a tale, in other words, whose progression is dialectical. As I have noted, we should try to assume the perspective of the Matengo, in which the first woman represents evil and the second represents good. The interplay of good and evil as dialectical opposites is sustained with remarkable skill. One is left in no doubt as to the ingenuity of the creators and performers of such tales. In this tale, good and evil as moral categories are personified, concretized, in the two women. the tale goes through several movements, each movement expressing a dialectic.

In the first movement, evil triumphs over good; the first woman's malicious plan to have the other woman pound her baby succeeds. In the second movement, good triumphs over evil: the second woman, by obtaining the beautiful babies, records a triumph greater than that of the first woman. It is a greater triumph, qualitatively and quantitatively. First, these new babies are much more beautiful than both her previous baby and the evil woman's baby. This is the qualitative aspect. Secondly, she obtains two babies as opposed to the one she lost; as opposed, even, to the one baby the other woman has. The second woman, personifying good, has thus been more than recompensed.

But this state of equilibrium is not permanent. The evil woman upsets it in her attempt to reassert her lost "glory." Her first attempt to do so, going in search of babies, fails. She does not get the kind of babies she was hoping for which would satisfy her ambitions. Her second attempt to assert herself, this time depriving the other woman of her children succeeds; thus, in the end, evil triumphs.

This tale deals with the theme of taboo violations. The killing of babies is taboo, and it is gruesome when done by mothers. Then the pounding of babies, sifting the four, and carrying it to the aunt as if it were food, has an explicit suggestion of cannibalism, another taboo subject. Only witches would do such a thing.

All the characters in this tale are witch-like: the aunt, the destitutes, and the two women. There are no men here, and this reinforces the idea that these are strange women, living alone, and doing their witchery.

After the tale has ended, we realize that poetic justice has not been achieved; the culprit is allowed to go unpunished. This fact, discomfiting as it may be, is not without its merits. It is an important instance of the realism we often find in oral literature. Oral literature reflects the contradictions in real life. Oral literature does not give us a melodramatic picture of life, wherein poetic justice is guaranteed. In oral literature, as in life itself, there is the interplay of both normal and abnormal situations and outcomes, the predictable and the unpredictable.

The dialectical strain of the tale manifests itself in other ways as well. I wish to focus on how the tale presents the character of the second woman. When the tale comes to a close, we can look back on it and note that the character of this woman has a contradictory aspect—the very goodness of her character is the cause of her undoing. Her innocent trust in other people brings about her ruin. Her goodness is at once her strong point and her weak point.

Still, this woman does not learn anything from her first misfortune. At the end of the tale, she still gives her children to the evil woman to take to the field, where she kills them. We wonder whether this woman, who seems so good, is really good or stupid.

The balance of the tale is sustained by contrast and repetition. First, there is the contrast between the character, actions, and fortunes of the two women. One woman pounds her child, the other doesn't; one helps the destitutes, the other doesn't; one obeys the aunt, the other doesn't; one obtains beautiful babies, the other doesn't.

Secondly, at the level of plot, we note a repetitive but contrastive pattern. One plot involves the trip of the second woman, which is a series of positive events. The second plot, involving the trip of the first woman, is a series of blunders. In folktales, we often come across this situation, whereby one character imitates what another character has done and fails to achieve the desired results, sometimes getting into trouble. This phenomenon is called unsuccessful repetition.

At the hands of a skillful performer, the tale achieves a harmonious blend of the tragic and the comic. The pathos surrounds the good woman, who has twice to bear the death of her babies. The most humorous incident is when the evil woman screams and yells in the hut as the various animals pay her a visit.

There are several abhorrent and fantastic elements in this tale, as is common in folk tales. The idea of pounding babies and sifting the flour is abhorrent. The way babies are obtained at the aunt's place is fantastic. For certain folklorists, especially those who believe in evolutionism, these abhorrent and fantastic elements are survivors from savage customs of the past.

However, it may not be easy to explain the fantastic elements in folktales. For one thing, they do not necessarily reflect social reality, past or present. They could be merely a product of human creative imagination. In oral literature, as in all art, imitation of life, or verisimilitude, is not always the goal. Truthfulness is, and has to be, sometimes sacrificed in order to achieve a particular effect or purpose.

Turning to the tale we are considering here, we may not know why and how the two women came upon the idea of pounding their babies, especially in view of the deep love mothers normally have for their babies. Still, this strange element appears in the tale and its function seems to be to set the narrative in motion in a striking way.

Another fantastic element in the tale is the power of human beings to understand the language of animals. In this tale, the aunt and the other people in her house listen to the cock and are able to understand what it is saying. The phenomenon of human beings talking to animals and vice versa is common is folklore all over the world. Stith Thompson notes:

> This trait is old and widespread in folklore and mythology. Siegfried in Norse myth and Melampus in Greek possessed this power, and they both received it from a serpent or dragon.[6]

Talking animals and communication between human beings and animals is an invention of human creative imagination. Gorky describes imagination these terms:

> Imagination is, in its essence, also a mode of thinking about the world, but thinking in terms of images. It may be said that imagination means the ability to attribute to things and to the elemental forces of nature human qualities, feelings and even intentions.
>
> We hear and speak of the wind "whining" or "moaning," the moon's "pensive light," a "babbling" brook, a "murmuring" stream and many other similar expressions, which are aimed at making natural phenomena more vivid.
>
> This is called anthropomorphism, from two Greek words: *anthropos*, which means man, and *morphe*, meaning form or image...There are people who think that anthropomorphism should have no place in literature, and even consider it detrimental to it, but these same people say "the frost pinched his ears," "the sun smiled," "May came round," and even speak of "villainous weather," though it would be hard to

---

[6] Stith Thompson, *The Folktale* (New York: Holt Rhinehart and Winston, 1949), p. 83

use a moral yardstick with reference to the weather.[7]

In this perspective, we can view the talking cock as being no more fantastic, qualitatively, than the biting frost. The mental frame required to produce both is the same, and the difference between the two fantastic elements is only one of degree, not of kind.

Finally, the problem of discussing fantastic elements is compounded since what is fantastic to a certain people may not be to others. We may judge an element in a folktale or a work of literature as fantastic, using our own standards or understanding, but we need to ask whether the people among whom the tale flourished think the same way. For people who believe in bird language, the talking cock is not fantastic.

---

[7] Maxim Gorky, *On Literature* (Moscow: Foreign Languages Press, n.d.), pp. 30-31.

Katigija

There was a man, and he bore two children. He left and went to the Coast. The children stayed with their grandmother and grandfather.

Now, the grandfather said this:

"You, Katigija, I am going to kill you."

When the grandmother heard this, she took Katigija and went and hid her at the *kijaniko*.[8] away from the house, at the place where the women spread out their foodstuffs to dry. She dug a small hole and put her in it and covered the hole.

Every day, in the evening, she sent the little girl some *ugali*.[9] Whenever she was sending the *ugali* to the little girl, the grandmother sang the following song:

> *Katigijou, ka-tija,*
> *Katigijou, ka-tija,*
> *Katigija, gu-bi kwako.*
> *Katigijou, ka-tija,*
> *Katigijou, ka-tija,*
> *Guhiki oti gukuli uwale.*

---

[8] *Kijaniko* is a place away from the house, where women spread out on mats various foodstuffs to dry. The word comes from the verb *kujanika*, means to spread out in order to dry. This applies also to the act of hanging out clothes to dry. But a *kijaniko* is not for clothes, only foodstuffs.

[9] The word *ugali* appears several times in this book. It can be spelled *ugwali* or *uwali*, or *uwale* or *ugwale*. Some of these differences come from variations in emphasis. The "i" suffix denotes the neutral form of the noun, while the "e" suffix denotes emphasis or some other kind of special impression. You can say *ugwali* to someone, or *uwali* and if they don't hear you, you say *ugwale* or *uwale* the second time, for emphasis. That is the way all Matengo nouns operate. There is always an emphatic or other form.

Katigijou, ka-tija,
Katigijou ka-tija,
Atati baku apiti ku-Mbwane;
Katigijou, ka-tija,
Katigijou, ka-tija.

Katigijou, ka-tijou,
Katigijou, ka-tijou,
Katigija, where are you.
Katigija, ka-tija,
Katigija, ka-tija,
Come, please, eat *u(g)wali*
Katigija, ka-tija,
Katigija, ka-tija,
Your father has gone to the Coast;
Katigija, ka-tija,
Katigija, ka-tija.

Then Katigija, who was in the hole, started to sing:

Katigijou, ka-tija,
Katigijou, ka-tija,
Natu a(n)heimbi kaboumba.
Katigijou, ka-tija,
Katigijou, ka-tija,
Natu annagani kungoma;
Katigijou, ka-tija,
Katigijou, ka-tija,
Natu biingoma mwei mmuto;
Katigijou, ka-tija,
Katigijou, ka-tija.

Katigija, ka-tija,
Katigija, ka-tija,
As for me, they have dug me a hole
Katigija, ka-tija,
Katigija, ka-tija,

As for me, they have plotted to kill me
Katigija, ka-tija,
Katigija, ka-tija,
As for me, they'll kill me when the moon is
    overhead
Katigija, ka-tija,
Katigija, ka-tija.

Then Katigija removed the lid-stone, and she got out. She was offered the *uwali* and she ate it. Then, the old woman told her to get back into the hole.

Now, the younger child started asking the old woman:

"Grandmother, where has Katigija gone?"

"Nobody knows," replied the old woman. "Where did you leave her?"

"Where is Katigija, Grandmother?" the child continued asking.

"At your aunt's," replied the grandmother.

The child went to her aunt's and failed to see Katigija. She returned.

"Grandmother, where is Katigija?"

"I don't know," said the old woman.

Now, one day, when the old woman was going out with the *uwali*, the child saw her. Another day the child, on her part, prepared some *uwali* and went out with it, singing:

> *Katigijou, ka-tija,*
> *Katigijou, ka-tija,*
> *Katigijou, gubi kwako?*
> *Katigijou, ka-tija,*
> *Katigijou ka-tija,*
> *Guhiki outi gukuli u(g)wale;*
> *Katigijaou ka-tija,*
> *Katigijaou ka-tija,*
> *Atati bitu atei kubouka.*

Katigijaou ka-tija,
Katigijaou ka-tija,
Atati bitu apiti ku-Mbwane;
Katigijou, ka-tija,
Katigijou, ka-tija.

Katigija, ka-tija,
Katigija, ka-tija,
Katigija, where are you?
Katigija, ka-tija,
Katigija, ka-tija,
Come, please, eat *uwali*
Katigija, ka-tija,
Katigija, ka-tija,
Our father went away
Katigija, ka-tija,
Katigija, ka-tija
Our father has gone to the Coast.
Katigija, ka-tija,
Katigija, ka-tija.

Katigija started singing:

Natu biindenda kungoma;
Katigijou, ka-tija,
Katigijou, ka-tija,
Natu anagani mwei mmuto.
Katigijou, ka-tija
Katigijou, ka-tija.

As for me, they are going to kill me.
Katigija, ka-tija,
Katigija, ka-tija,
As for me, their secret plot is when the moon is
    overhead
Katigija, ka-tija,
Katigija, ka-tija.

Katigija got out of the hole, ate the *uwali*, and returned into the hole.

Then, the father came from the Coast. He said:

"Our Old Lady, where has Katigija gone?"

"I don't know," said the old woman.

The father then asked the old man:

"Our Old Man, where is Katigija?"

"She has gone to her aunt's," said the old man.

The father went to the aunt's, and there he was told that Katigija was not there.

The father returned. He again asked the old man:

"Our Old Man, where is Katigija?"

"I don't know," said the old man.

Meanwhile, the old woman prepared some *uwali* and went out to the same place in the bush:

> *Katigijou, ka-tija,*
> *Katigijou, ka-tija,*
> *Guhiki outi gukuli uwale*
> *Katigijou, ka-tija,*
> *Katigijou, ka-tija,*
> *Atati baku heinu ahikite;*
> *Katigijaou, ka-tija,*
> *Katigijaou kati-ja.*
>
> *Katigija, ka-tija,*
> *Katigija, ka-tija,*
> Come, please, eat *uwali.*
> *Katigija, ka-tija,*
> *Katigija, ka-tija,*
> Your father has now come;
> *Katigija, ka-tija,*
> *Katigija, ka-tija.*

From the hole, Katigija started singing:

Katigijou, ka-tija,
Katigijou, ka-tija,
Natu annagani kungoma
Katigijou, ka-tija,
Katigijaou ka-tija,
Natu biingoma mwei mmuto
Katigijou, ka-tija,
Katigijou, ka-tija.

Katigija, ka-tija,
Katigija, ka-tija,
As for me, they have plotted to kill me
Katigija, ka-tija,
Katigija, ka-tija,
As for me, their plot is when the moon is
    overhead
Katigija, ka-tija,
Katigija, ka-tija.

She came out, ate the *uwali,* and returned into the hole, and she was covered up again.

The old woman went back to the house.

"Old man," the father started again, "where has Katigija gone?"

"She is at her uncle's. Follow her there."

The man went to the uncle's.

"Katigija is not here," they told him.

He returned.

"Old man," he asked, "where is Katigija?"

"She has gone to her sister's," said the old man.

The father went to the sister's and did not find Katigija there.

As he was returning home, the father decided he was going to kill the old man. He came home and killed the old man.

Then, the old woman told him:

"Katigija had been earmarked for death by her grandfather. I went and dug a hole at the *kijaniko*, in which I hid her. Let me go and bring her out."

The old woman went and brought out Katigija.

Katigija came back and the old woman stayed. And here ends the tale.

Comments on
Katigija

I have titled this tale "Katigija" because Katigija is the focal point of the tale. Katigija is the centre towards which all the threads of the tale lead and around which they spin.

This is a moving, sorrowful tale. The plight of the little girl, Katigija; the anxiety of her fellow child; and the anguish of the nameless man, their father, are some of the most sensitive points of this seemingly simple but powerful tale. Fortunately, as if to mitigate the sorrow we might feel, the tale finally resolves the tension it has built up, in the classical manner of melodrama: crime is punished and innocence vindicated.

The departure of the man for the Coast ushers in the subsequent chain of events. His departure, or, more accurately, his absence, provides the old man with the occasion to attempt effecting his wicked plan to kill Katigija. The old man discloses his diabolical plan to the little, innocent Katigija in a manner that is blunt, stone-hearted, and harrowing: "You, Katigija, I am going to kill you!"

Nothing could be more callous and inhuman than this statement, made to a mere child. It chills the blood.

Apparently, the old man's statement was made within the hearing of the old woman, Katigija's grandmother. This old woman is very kind. She is the one who saves Katigija's life. Yet, there are certain aspects of her behaviour that seem to be negative. Why did this old woman not tell the other child the whereabouts of Katigija when this child asked her? Why did she deliberately lie to the child, first telling her that nobody knew where Katigija was, then telling her that she was at her aunt's, and finally that she didn't know where Katigija was? Why did she tell Katigija's father, worried and anguished as he was, that she did not know where Katigija was? If she had told the man the truth at once, would this not have saved him the great and prolonged anguish he suffered as he moved from place to place in search of the little girl? Was it kindness to hide the truth from this poor suffering man or was it cruelty? These are difficult questions, and perhaps it is not quite right to say that this old woman is very kind.

We can, perhaps, still justify the old woman, relying on extrinsic standards rather than evidence from the tale itself. Would it have been wise for the old woman to tell a small child the terrible truth about Katigija's fate? After all, in Matengo culture, children are not told the truth regarding such phenomena as birth and death. When children ask where babies come from, they are told that babies are fished out of rivers. With the coming of Christian missionaries, children are also told that babies are bought from the sisters at the mission centre. When someone dies, children may at most be told that the person has been taken away by *lindu*, an unspecified monster. In view of this, we could say that in withholding from the child the truth about Katigija's whereabouts, the old woman was acting in an appropriate manner.

Nevertheless, it is still difficult to explain why she did the same to Katigija's father. Did this man, a grown up and Katigija's parent, deserve the same treatment as the child? Why did the old woman fail to tell this man the truth?

We have little information from the tale to help us answer these questions. We can only use our common sense or engage in speculations. We could speculate that it would not have been sensible to disclose to this man the whole story about the plot on Katigija's life. A violent quarrel, even a murder, might have ensued. Perhaps the old woman was fearing that if she told Katigija's father about the plot, he might go and kill the old man. The old woman may have been guided by the thought that as long as Katigija was alive, there was no need to create a situation that might lead to violence and murder. Perhaps, in other words, the old woman acted wisely in withholding the truth from Katigija's father.

Unfortunately, perhaps fortunately, the old man is killed, anyway. Now, with the old man out of the way, it would seem that this is the right time for the old woman to tell Katigija's father the truth about Katigija's plight. The man has found out for himself that the old man was evil and did not deserve to live. In this context, what the old woman has to tell him only confirms the man's independent discovery. Perhaps it would not have been quite proper for the old woman to tell the man the evils of the old man when he asked about Katigija. Any rational person would guard against behaving like a reckless tale-bearer.

What is significant is that, when we think carefully about this tale, it raises many difficult questions. It appears that the old woman is a life-affirming character. She saves Katigija and makes sure that the little girl is provided with food all the time she is hiding in the hole. She also seems, as I have speculated, to be trying to refrain from saying or doing anything that might lead to conflict or loss of life; however, this old woman is not really prepared to defend or save the lives of those who deny others the right to live. That is why she does not actively try to save the life of the evil old man, nor, to cap it all, does she mourn his death.

Katigija's father is presented as a man of few words, a man of integrity. He is also very patient. It is only as a last resort, when his patience has been exhausted, that he decides to kill the old man. By means of this act, justice is done, to the relief of all of us. We do not and need not feel the slightest pity for this old man. The tale has built up such an image of him that we cannot but consider him the incarnation of evil, and as a result of this psychological preparation, we take his death as some kind of much-needed exorcism. A devil has been expelled from our midst. The death of the old man is an act of purgation; it purges the emotions of fear and pity that the tale has built up in the audience. If the old man was an agent of destruction in this house, his death rids the house of this dangerous denizen, bringing to it peace once again. At this point, appropriately, Katigija can now return from her exile, as it were, to live in this atmosphere of peace.

We are told at the very beginning of this tale that the man, Katigija's father, left home and went to the Coast. This information is sure to strike a deep note in the hearts of a Matengo audience. It brings to mind memories of the colonial era. Throughout the colonial period, many Matengo able-bodied men were forced to leave home and go to distant places in search of "paid" employment. In those days, money was scarce, and one had to work very hard to get it. The colonial government imposed taxes on the people, forcing them to go in search of money. Failing to pay tax was a serious crime, and the colonial government dealt ruthlessly with people who failed to pay tax. People also needed money to buy commodities (such as cloth, utensils, and salt) that were increasingly becoming necessities.

So, many Matengo left home and went to distant places to look for money and the things that money could buy. They went to Central and Southern Africa to work in such places as the Copperbelt in what is today Zambia and the Rand in what is today South Africa. Others went to the coastal areas of East Africa to work mainly in sisal plantations.

Some of those who went to these places never returned, and we do not know whether they are alive or dead. Those who did return brought with them symbols of "civilization" such as blankets, hats, and neck-ties. From time to time, even today, someone leaves Matengoland and goes to the Coast to bring back a long lost relative. When the prodigal arrives in the Matengo highlands, he is made the subject of lively and often derisive gossip. Nevertheless, these people who went to the Coast and came back continue to enthrall audiences with their tales of wonder and adventure in foreign lands.

The plot of this tale is very simple, and the narrative is straightforward. What sets the tale in motion is the murder plot hatched by the old man. What follows is the old woman's successful attempt to foil this plot.

With the arrival of the man from the Coast, the tale branches into two plots which run concurrently but parallel to each other. There is the plot involving the way the old woman is maintaining the little girl in the hole, and there is the plot involving the father's anxious search for Katigija. When the tale ends, we cannot but admire the skill and success with which the confluence and resolution of the two plots is brought about.

Repetition is a key structural device in this tale. The song is repeated many times, with slight variation, but the same tune. In the original Matengo, the song is sorrowful; its being repeated so many times underlines the pervasive sadness of the tale.

This is not the only instance of repetition or the only repeated element. The child asks the old woman the same kinds of questions that Katigija's father later asks her. The sequence of questions and answers is similar; the person asking wants to know where Katigija is, and the old woman gives the same evasive answers. This generates and sustains suspense. It also makes us impatient; we want to know what happens next, but the tale inches forward slowly, as if to ensure that we have securely grasped and internalized each of its details.

Nokamboka and the Baby Monster

There was a man. He had no child. He just lived like that—childless.

Now, he set out to till his *kijoungu*.[10] He hoed and hoed. Then he came across a strange creature, not big, but small. He picked it up. He took it home and covered it in a pot. Now, after he had covered it in the pot, he stayed for a long time. When he went to uncover the pot, the creature had grown. When the monster had thus grown, the man went out to attend an initiation dance. The monster followed, singing:

> *Mpwaga lindu, lindu nye-nye,*
> *Tuli lindu, lindu nye-nye*
> *Nipala ba-Nokamboka nye-nye*
> *Tuli lindu, lindu nye-nye*
> *Bandoi Ku'nkouka nye-nye*
> *Tuli lindu lindu nye-nye,*
> *Tulii,*
> *Nye-nye tulii,*
> *Nyee, nye-nye tulii*

> You say I'm a monster,
> A monster, a monster;
> I'm after Nokamboka,
> A monster, a monster
> He dared take me from the lowlands

---

[10] A *kijoungu* is a well-watered plot of land in a valley used for growing crops. The land is so well watered that drainage channels are dug to get rid of the excess water. The usual crops grown in a *kijoungu* are pumpkins, maize, and beans.

A monster, a monster.

People who were dancing at the initiation ceremony said:

"You, Nokamboka, you are being called this way."

"Who is looking for me?" Nokamboka asked.

"Come and recognize him yourself," they told him.

So, poor Nokamboka got out only to come face to face with the monster, which was fully armed with such weapons as spears and pangas, intending to use them for killing Nokamboka.

Poor Nokamboka took to his heels and flew homewards. He climbed to the attic to hide.

The monster followed him, singing:

> *Mpwaga lindu, lindu nye-nye*
> *Tuli lindu, lindu nye-nye;*
> *Bandoi, Ku'nkouka nye-nye,*
> *Tuli lindu, lindu nye-nye;*
> *Nitakutia mkuki nye-nye;*[11]
> *Tuli lindu, lindu nye-nye*
> *Tulii,*
> *Nyee, nye-nye tulii.*

You say I'm a monster,
A monster, a monster;
He dared take me from the lowlands,
A monster, a monster,
I'm going to spear you,
A monster, a monster.

---

[11] This statement in the song, *Nitakutia mkuki*, is in Swahili, not Matengo, like the rest of the song. It means "I am going to spear you." It is an interesting case of code switching, and one wonders what the original Matengo statement may have been.

And the monster, on its part, climbed to the attic. It pulled Nokamboka down to the floor and killed him.

The end of the tale.

Nokamboka and the Baby Monster

This is the tragedy of a man who, condemned to childlessness, stumbles across a young creature and takes it home as a kind-hearted person would take an orphan baby. Yet, very unfortunately, what Nokamboka may have innocently believed to be an act of kindness and compassion turns out to have been a tragic error, an error that costs him his life. As a result of this error, Nokamboka suffers an untimely and cruel death at the hands of the very creature he has done so much to preserve and protect.

One has to see this tale against the background of African cultures and the great value those cultures place on children. Africans desire children. When a person grows up, he or she is expected to marry and have children. The first obligation after a couple gets married is to have a child, and it is necessary that the child should come within the first year. Otherwise, everybody starts worrying. This cultural pattern appears again and again in African folktales. Among the most tragic figures in African folktales is the person who fails to have a child. In these tales, such a person struggles desperately to seek remedies for this problem, through consulting healers or any other agencies.

The man in this tale draws the sympathy of the audience because he is childless. However, the fact that he is alone is another sad element in the tale. Africans assume that everybody who has reached a certain age must be married. They also assume that anybody who is not married must be very unhappy. On a more general sense, they also take it for granted that everybody must live as part of a community: a family, a clan, a village, and so forth. The idea of a person living alone is disturbing.

This tale raises troublesome questions. Does kindness deserve such a reward? Would it have been better for Nokamboka to leave the creature where he found it? Was Nokamboka foolish to pick up something he did not know? We may have different answers to these questions. Still, it seems really sad that this unfortunate man, who had no children and who therefore felt he had found something that he could take care of and bring up like a child, ends up losing his life. This is terrifying.

I have called the tale a tragedy. It is the nature of tragedy that a person *like us* incurs suffering through an error of judgment, thereby arousing both pity and fear in us, the people who witness or hear about the matter. As M.H. Abrams put it, following Aristotle, "The tragic hero moves us to pity because, since he is not an evil man, his misfortune is greater than he deserves; but he moves us also to fear, because we recognize similar possibilities of error in our own lesser and fallible selves."[12] In other words, we could ourselves make a similar mistake and suffer similar consequences.

Of course, we may not ourselves have the ill luck in our lifetime to stumble across a young monster, but we could be fated to go through a similar experience, albeit in a less fantastic form than Nokamboka's encounter with the monster. The tale makes us

---

[12] M.H. Abrams, *A Glossary of Literary Terms* (New York; Holt Rinehart and Winston, 1993), pp. 212-213.

remember the times we have experienced or witnessed kindness being rewarded with evil deeds. It reminds us of experiences where innocent mistakes have produced disastrous consequences.

It would appear that in this tragedy, Nokamboka stands alone, a solitary individual confronting an inscrutable but cruel Fate. Fate has denied him the joy and company of children and a family. From an African point of view, this is enough of a problem. Nokamboka, worse still, does not seem to have good connections with the people around him. When, at the initiation dance, he is told that someone is looking for him, the people shrug him off with the words: "Come and recognize him yourself." Nokamboka is an alienated individual.

Nokamboka's alienation, nevertheless, is a specific, personal situation. The tale does not, on the basis of Nokamboka's predicament, make generalizations about life. It does not express the view, popularized by certain existentialist philosophers, that alienation is an integral part of the human condition.

The people at the dance say, "Come and recognize him yourself." There is something disturbing about these remarks. In a way we cannot explain, these people seem to be refusing to have anything to do with Nokamboka's fate. Have they sensed the impending tragedy? We do not know, and perhaps we cannot know.

The power of this tale resides in part in its mysteries, which leave us intrigued, afraid, and without answers.

Postscript—
Notes on the
Folktale

The folktale is a well known type of narrative, found all over the world. It is also very old. The oldest folktales we know come from ancient Egypt, such as the "Tale of the Shipwrecked Sailor" and "The Tale of the Two Brothers."[13]

It is not easy to define the folktale. We use the term to describe quite different kinds of narrative. In addition, every society has its own name for the kind of narrative we call a folktale. It would be best, therefore, to call these narratives by their local names. The Matengo call these narratives *ihoumu*, the singular being *luhoumu*,[14] with the stress on "*i*" and "*lu*" respectively. The word comes from the verb *kuhouma*, which means to stitch. Still, the term folktale is handy and common.

Folktales often share themes, episodes, characters, or structural features. Nevertheless, some tales are more complex than others in structure or theme; some are long, and some are short. However, we have to be

---

[13]For this information, see Stith Thompson, *The Folktale* (New York: The Dryden Press, 1946), pp. 273-276. The "Tale of the Shipwrecked Sailor" is printed in, for example, *The Norton Anthology, Expanded Edition*, Vol. 1., ed. Maynard Mack (New York: W.W. Norton & Company, 1995), pp. 51-55. "The Tale of the Two Brothers" is published in *Egyptian Tales*, edited by William Matthew Flinders Petrie (London: Methuen, 1895), pp. 36-65, and in Harold Scheub, *The African Storyteller* (Dubuque, Iowa: Kendall/Hunt Publishing Company, 1990), pp. 375-382.

[14]The "*ou*" sound in this word should be pronounced like the "oa" in "boat."

careful when we use concepts like long and short to describe these narratives. We have to remember that the original and natural mode of existence of these tales is oral performance. Often, what appears to be a short tale on paper may take a long time to perform before an audience. The story teller can lengthen or shorten the tale by adding or omitting details, varying the tempo of performance, and repeating or abbreviating certain elements. It is thus difficult to say, from looking at the text on a page, how short or long a tale is or can be.

The same caution applies to songs. Printed on a page, a song may seem short. In performance, however, it can last a long time, the same words or phrases being repeated, over and over. It is thus not possible to say whether a song is short or long by merely looking at a song text on a page.

Matengo folktales do not have fixed titles. This is true of African tales in general. Each story teller, each audience, is free to label the tale the way they find suitable as long as the label identifies the tale and distinguishes it from other tales. The normal way of naming such tales is to mention a memorable incident in the tale. The tale which I have called "The Tale of Two Women" might be referred to by the Matengo as "that tale in which they lick wounds," or "that tale in which they pound babies." It is conceivable, therefore, that different titles could be used for the same tale by different people or by the same people on different occasions.

When we write down or publish such tales, we give them titles, as I have done in this book. These titles are fixed, creating the false impression that they are the titles assigned to these tales in their original communities. We have to be aware of this issue; it highlights one of the consequences, and perhaps dangers, of textualizing tales.

The larger problem, of course, is that the written text of a tale does not really correspond to the tale in its natural form, which is oral performance. The natural mode of existence of a tale is oral performance. In this mode, the tale is not fixed, the way the written text is fixed. In fact, we can even ask whether the tale exists at all when it is not being performed or after it is performed. When the performance is over, does the tale still exist? If it does, in what form? We cannot say that everything disappears, since people still remember "that tale in which they pound babies" or "that tale in which they lick wounds." That is why they can tell it. Something surely exists in the minds of the story tellers and the audience, but what exactly is it? This is a question to think about.

The origins of folktales is another intriguing issue. Where did these tales come from? Who created them, and when? Basically, we do not know the answers to these questions. We can assume, however, that there was an individual or a group of individuals who created each tale. One individual may have created the initial version, the rudiments of the tale, or one of the episodes of the tale, and other people then modified and elaborated on it as they told and retold it, adding more episodes to it; thus creating a complete or complex tale.

In the final analysis, the tale is a product of both individual and collective creativity. This process continues today, as tales get told and retold by different people. In this process, the tales get changed in certain ways. Typically, elements from contemporary life get incorporated into the tales. One should not be surprised, for example, if a modern storyteller says that Hare walked around the village carrying a radio.

Sometimes people have claimed that folktales are a product of communal creativity, as if to imply that there is no individual authorship. As I have suggested, it seems best to view the process as a dialectical one involving both individual and collective creativity.

We need to ask, however, whether new tales are being created or whether people are only telling and modifying the old tales. I think this is an interesting question. Studies suggest that there is only a limited set of tale types and plot elements. All tales draw from only that limited set of plot elements. Vladimir Propp called these elements functions.[15] A function, he wrote, "is understood as an act of a character, defined from the point of view of its significance for the course of the action." He went on to say that "[f]unctions of characters serve as stable, constant elements in a tale, independent of how and by whom they are fulfilled. They constitute the fundamental components of a tale," and that "[t]he number of functions known to the fairy tale is limited." He noted that no matter which elements or functions a tale incorporates, their sequence in the tale (which make up what he called the morphology of the tale) remains constant.[16]

If we look at three of the functions described by Propp: (1) one of the members of a family absents himself from home, (2) an interdiction is addressed to the hero, (3) the interdiction is violated,[17] we can see what he means. The interdiction, whether a command

---

[15]Vladimir Propp. *The Morphology of the Folktale*, trans. Laurence Scott (Austin: University of Texas Press, 1968).

[16]Propp, pp. 21-24.

[17]Propp, pp. 26-27.

or a prohibition must come before the violation in any tale that incorporates those two functions. Let us look at another list of functions from Propp: (1) the hero leaves home, (2) the hero is tested, interrogated, attacked, etc., which prepares the way for his receiving either a magical agent or helper, (3) the hero reacts to the actions of the future donor, (4) the hero acquires the use of a magical agent.[18] Again, according to Propp, that sequence is the same in any tale that contains those functions. In fact, the "Tale of Two Women" in my collection supports Propp's point.

Using Propp's theory, it does not seem possible to create new tale plots. Whether the tale is told as a novel, a movie, or a play, it cannot invent any new plot; we can say it is necessarily a retelling of some old tale. Thus the story of Oedipus may appear in an ancient Greek myth, in a Shakespeare play, or in a modern movie. I find this theory interesting, since I can see that the same conflicts, themes, and character types continue to appear in tales that have been around since time immemorial. In that sense, I think we are not able to create new tales. If we are telling the story of a hero, for example, we can see many such stories have already been told.

Another thing that has fascinated and intrigued scholars is the existence of similar tales in various parts of the world. The famous tale of Cinderella, for example, has analogues in different parts of the world.[19] How did this come about?

At least two theories have been proposed. One theory is that tales spread from one place to another. This process is called diffusion, and it is easy to

[18]Propp, pp. 39-43.
[19]For global studies of this tale, see Alan Dundes, *Cinderella, a Casebook* (Madison: University of Wisconsin Press, 1988).

understand how this process works. As people travel or migrate from one place to another, they are likely to carry their tales with them and introduce them to other communities.

The other theory proposes what is called polygenesis or multiple origins. The tales may have been created in different parts of the world independently. Because human beings are the same, they have the same ability to create tales. We have the same capacity for imagination, which enables us to create tales.

Some of the people who believe in polygenesis rely on theories about dreams. These theories have been developed especially by those who work in the tradition of psychoanalysis. Their studies show that the themes and events in the dreams of human beings all over the world are strikingly similar. Dreams are a key source of the motifs and other elements we encounter in folktales; thus, the connection between dreams and folktale motifs helps to explain the similarity between folktales across the world.

We also see similarities in folktales across the world because people all over the world have similar experiences, such as love and conflict. It is thus logical that people in different parts of the world would come up with similar folktales. In other words, social life itself is the source of folktales.

To understand the origin of Matengo tales, we need to take into account all these factors. The Matengo are a collection of clans that came from different directions at different times into the area they inhabit today. Some clans came from the south, perhaps Mozambique or even further south; others came from the north, and others from Malawi, to the west. It is logical to assume that at least some of the tales we call Matengo tales came from these places.

Considering all this, we may have to ask whether it makes sense to call these tales Matengo tales. In what sense are they Matengo tales if they may have been brought into Matengo society from so many other communities? Maybe that is not a problem. We can say that these tales are Matengo because, irrespective of their origins, they are an integral part of Matengo folklore and culture.

We can use the analogy of language to clarify the argument. Just as a language incorporates words and other elements from other languages without losing its identity, the folklore of a given group also incorporates elements from different sources without losing its identity.

Why do people tell tales? What is the function of these tales? These questions are important, and many people have tried to answer them. One of the most common assumptions is that folktales educate and entertain children. I am not sure I agree with this view completely. I grew up in a society where folktales were a living reality. During the telling of tales, usually people of all ages were present, and they all enjoyed the tales. In addition, everybody was free to tell tales.

One function of these tales is to entertain, of course. Many tales are pleasant, funny, and entertaining. Also, many tales involve audience participation in singing, which can be a pleasant form of entertainment in its own right. In addition, the context of storytelling is often a broader one in which other kinds of entertainment are involved, such as telling jokes, drumming, hand-clapping, and even dancing. It is a mistake to imagine the telling of tales as an isolated activity during which nothing else happens.

Some tales deal with ethical or moral questions, and are meant to educate, challenge, or provoke the intellectual powers of the audience. In this respect, tales challenge adult minds as well. The trickster tale is perhaps the best example of this. The trickster mocks, challenges, or subverts accepted norms and values. In this way, he or she tests them. Through such testing, the trickster helps to define, maintain, and strengthen the existing norms and values. Often, the best way to strengthen something is by subjecting it to stress or pressure of some kind.[20]

Since the trickster also leads us into a world beyond the acceptable norms, he or she enables us to imagine alternatives to the world we are familiar with. The trickster enables us to contemplate other modes of being or doing things, no matter how fantastic or outrageous. This, in itself, can be intellectually stimulating.

When are tales told? In many books about folktales, we read that folk tales are told after the evening meal, around the fireside. Most people take this idea for granted. They have internalized the popular image of Africans working the whole day, congregating in the evening for the evening meal, and then story telling around the fireside. This is a simplistic view which I have called the fireside stereotype of African storytelling.[21]

First, it is not true that Africans everywhere work the whole day. There are many parts of Africa which are too hot for that. People in those parts might work in the morning and rest during the remainder of the

[20]For additional statements along these lines, see Joseph L. Mbele, "Review of 'Sacred Buffalo People,' a video on Native American culture and folklore," *Multicultural Education*, 2, 4 (1995), pp. 36-37.
[21]I introduced this phrase in my paper, "Oral Literature Scholarship as an Arena of Ideological Struggle," presented at the Second Ibadan Annual African Literature Conference, Ibadan, Nigeria, July 1977.

day. It is possible these people tell stories during the part of the day when they are not working.

Second, in these warm parts of Africa, it is not likely that people sit around the fire in the evening. If they need to tell stories at all, they surely sit somewhere, but it cannot be around a fire.

Third, there are people in Africa who do not have the guarantee of an evening meal. They may sometimes go without. This does not prevent them from telling and listening to tales.

The Matengo, however, do sit around the fire in the evening, because their land is cold for much of the year. Here the idea of tales told around the fireside applies. There are many other people in Africa who are in the same situation as the Matengo, but such cases do not legitimize the widespread fireside stereotype of African story telling.

There are no professional story tellers among the Matengo. There are people who are considered good story tellers, but they are not professionals; they do not make a living by telling tales, as is the case in some other parts of Africa and elsewhere. Among the Matengo, everyone is expected to be able to tell a story, although levels of competence differ from one person to the next. When people gather to tell tales, they will listen to anyone who has a tale to tell. Even children get a chance to tell tales in such gatherings. That is how they learn. Some of the tales in this book were told by very young people—barely in their teens—both male and female.

When the tales are told, there is always an audience. The members of the audience are not passive; they respond to the tales in various ways. They laugh when the story is funny; they express sorrow if the story is sad; they participate in singing the songs. If the audience shows much interest in the story, the story teller feels encouraged to prolong and embellish it; if the audience is not responsive, the story teller may shorten the tale. There is thus a close interaction between the story teller and the audience. In fact, the audience helps to determine the nature of the tale.

As I have noted above, there is no clear cut distinction between audience and storyteller. Members of the audience can and do tell stories. People take turns to tell stories, and even children are encouraged to try their hand at telling stories.

Some tales contain songs and chants. Songs and chants have various functions, depending on the tale. In the tale "Hawk and Crow," we see Hawk singing as he goes from homestead to homestead, looking for Crow and the chicks. The song she sings is a commentary on the Crows. It judges them, calling them half-wits. In the tale "Hare and the Great Drought," Hare sings a song about his xylophone, which not only tells about the xylophone but also adds flavour to the tale as such. In the original Matengo, this is a very pleasant song.

The songs give a special quality and flavour to the tales. They give the audience the chance to be active participants through singing, hand-clapping, and playing instruments. When my father told tales at home, my brothers, my sisters, and I would join in the singing; we would clap hands, take a stick and beat a stool, a pan, or anything to provide the rhythm. Songs increase the artistic appeal of the tale.

In the tale of Katigija, the old woman sings a song that she repeats many times with some modifications. In fact, the song seems to be as important as the tale itself. In its own way, the song retells the tale, summarizing it and reinforcing its message.

In the tale of Nokamboka, we have songs that function in the same way, essentially. The first song the little monster sings retells the tale. The second, whose tune is the same as the first, retells the tale and declares the monster's intention to kill Nokamboka. In this way, the songs both recall and retell the tale. The second song goes further and anticipates the action of the tale.

Certain scholars have noted that the songs in folktales are very old. They are among the oldest elements in the tales, having been passed on from generation to generation with few changes, if any. During the telling of the tale, the sentences, phrases and other elements can change easily; however, the song tends to remain the same. This is because the song tends to be rhythmical, economical, and easily remembered. Songs are thus among the most stable elements in a tale because they are difficult to change and easy to remember. Rhythm, rhyme, meter, and other resources are the devices that facilitate memorization and recall. All such resources that aid memorization are called mnemonic devices.

In "Hawk and Crow," we hear the chant by Chameleon as he tries to find Crow's whereabouts. This chant or incantation is a divination formula and is meant to work magic. If you have attended a magic show, you may have heard the magician saying strange words. A formula, a statement, or a chant that is used in these situations is called an abracadabra. Chameleon's chant in this tale is an abracadabra.

Often, it is very difficult for us to tell the meaning of the songs and chants. They contain words that we no longer use or know. In fact, the whole song may consist of incomprehensible words.

It is not accurate, however, to conclude that these songs and chants are meaningless. Folktales and other forms of folklore contain not only songs but other elements whose meanings we cannot figure out. Some people have referred to them as "nonsense words" or "nonsense syllables." This is not accurate. We may not be able to say what these elements mean, but we cannot deny that they have much musical, rhythmic, metrical, and artistic meaning and much emotional power.

Some of these elements are ideophones, which evoke moods or actions. The sound *"Mbombombombombombo"* in the "Tale of Two Women" is very significant to a Matengo audience. It imitates the sound of something falling down, as through a metal pipe.

We often think about the relationship of tales to social life. Most people assume that folktales reflect social reality. This is true to a certain extent and in the case of certain tales; however, some tales go beyond social realities and engage in speculations. "How Hare Helped Civet" raises the idea of a male giving birth. In real life, this does not happen, but in the realm of intellectual speculation and imagination, it is possible. In this tale, we are able to ask ourselves what would happen if men could conceive and give birth. Like science fiction, folktales often transcend social realities and often anticipate social realities. In other words, folktales may deal with realities that are beyond life as we know it and can deal with realities that may come to be.

Tales may reflect social life or aspects of social life; however, they also scrutinize, question, challenge, or contradict social realities. The tale is a world of its own, quite separate from the real world of the tellers and audiences. In this special world of the tale, tellers and audiences are free to pose questions, explore relationships, and make speculations that may not accord with the norms of actual social life. There is much freedom in this fictional world of the tale that may not be available or possible in actual life. The dimensions of this freedom are many. Impossible things happen; for example, animals talking with human beings, children growing up the moment they are born, or the mummy of an antelope getting back to life and engaging in the adventures we hear about in "Hare, Civet and Antelope."

Most people take for granted that folktales contain the wisdom of the society, that folktales transmit this wisdom from one generation to the next. This is true to some degree; however, this view tends to degenerate into another romantic notion about folktales, and we need to consider this view carefully: there is no society that produces only wisdom. The content of the folktales and other folklore of a society is complex; it contains not only the wisdom but also the folly of the society. They contain and project the hopes, anxieties, triumphs, failures, good, evil, dreams, and nightmares of the society.

The tales in this collection were told in Matengo. The English versions presented here are quite different from the originals because there are several main problems in translating tales. First, the meaning of words in one language cannot really be expressed in another language. There is always some difference, and something is either lost, gained, or missed in translation. A translation is not identical to the original. In fact, a translation is inevitably a new work. Put more bluntly, there is no such thing as a translation.

Next, like many African languages, Matengo has sounds with particular connotations or musical values for which there are no equivalents in English. I have mentioned ideophones, for example. There are also whole expressions whose meanings even the Matengo do not know, especially in songs. How does one translate these into English? There is no satisfactory answer to this question.

In addition, these tales were performed orally; they had the typical features of oral delivery, such as incomplete sentences, false starts, hesitation phenomena, and ungrammatical expressions. Often the storyteller would make a false start or statement and then correct it. Sometimes a member of the audience would ask the storyteller to repeat or clarify something and he or she would do so. The question one faces is whether the translations should follow the pattern of the originals, reflecting all these features faithfully, or whether one is allowed to make changes. In a text prepared for scholars, one has to follow the original faithfully, and I plan to do so in the future. This version of the tales, however, is an introductory work for general readership.

If one follows the original faithfully, that is, if one makes a literal translation, the result is bound to be awkward English because the structure of Matengo is different from that of English. Let us take the following Matengo sentence: *"Le liindu leela litei kubouka."* A literal translation of this sentence would be, "That monster that one has done to go." A translation in proper English would be "That monster then went away." In translating a folktale, one has to make choices between these possibilities. In their book *The Mwindo Epic*, Daniel Biebuyck and Kahombo Mateene try in their English translation to maintain some of the flavour of the original Nyanga language.[22]

---

[22] Daniel Biebuyck and Kahombo C. Mateene, *The Mwindo Epic* (Berkeley: University of California Press, 1969).

In my translations, I have tried to render the tales in readable English while maintaining the spirit of the original Matengo. Here are some examples: on the tape, the tale of Katigija starts this way:

Jwabya mundo; jwabya na bana abeili. Mweni jwajenda kumbwani.

A word-for-word translation of this would be: "There was a person; he/she was with children two. He/she himself/herself was going and was gone to the Coast."

In this book, I have rendered this section as: "There was a man, and he bore two children. He left and went to the Coast."

You can see the changes I have introduced, including identifying the person as male. In the original Matengo, it is not possible to say, at least up to this point, whether the person was male or female. The noun *mundu* (or *mundo*) meaning person, is the same for a male and a female person.

Another sentence, which comes at the beginning of this tale is "*GwaKatigija we ne mwitinugutenda kugukoma.*" A word for word translation translation of this would be: "You, Katigija, you I am going to do you to kill you." In this book, I have rendered this statement as "You, Katigija, I am going to kill you."

The tales were told orally. How does one write them down? How, in other words, does one transform an oral tale into a text? The oral tale is not just a string of words. It incorporates many elements which are not words, such as gestures and music. Even the words that are spoken can be spoken loud or in a whisper, fast or slowly. How do we represent these features on a page? Then, a story teller may use pauses to achieve special effects such as suspense. How do we represent these on the page?

There have been some ideas about how to solve these problems of textualizing oral performances, but there has not been a consensus. The issue is still problematical. Writing about the tales of the Fipa of Western Tanzania, Willis notes:

> Obviously the presentation in print of such a volatile art presents peculiar problems. Perhaps the best way to convey most immediately to the reader an idea of the communal creation of Fipa stories, and the fundamental sense in which the group context works on the form and content of artistic productions, is to exploit the frequently drawn parallel between spoken art and drama and present a translated excerpt from a typical story-telling session as a theatrical script, complete with stage directions.[23]

Other people have suggested that we should represent loud phrases or words with capital letters. Some suggest that we should indicate pauses with dots. All these are improvisations, and there is no standard system accepted by everybody.

The textualization of oral traditions affects our understanding of those traditions. The written word, in general, tends to be seen as authoritative. When a tale is rendered in written form, we tend to regard the text as the correct or authoritative version. We tend to forget that the writing down of a tale does not remove the tale from the community in which we recorded it. The tales flourish in that community even after we have recorded and published them. What we record and publish is just one performance of the tale. The tale can never be performed in the same way again.

---

[23] Roy Willis, *There was a Certain Man: Spoken Art of the Fipa* (Oxford: Oxford University Press, 1978), p. 22.

The character of each performance, and therefore of each resulting text, depends on the occasion on which it was done, the mood or competence of the narrator, the nature and disposition of the audience, and the location. With all these considerations in mind, we must acknowledge that no performance can be identical to another.

Let us use a simple example. If we take a narrator to a television station, he or she may be nervous and narrate the tales or sing the songs in a manner that reflects that condition; however, if the same narrator is at home, among family members and neighbors, he or she is likely to narrate and sing in a different manner.

Tales also change because of the memory of the narrator, the demands and exigencies of the audience, and so forth.

The basic point is that in their natural context, tales are not fixed the way the texts we publish are fixed. Fluidity rather than fixity is the natural mode of oral tales. Published tales generate the idea of fixity.

Many collectors of the tales from African societies were missionaries or colonial officials and anthropologists. The presence of such a person in an African community was bound to have a great effect on the kind of material that could be recorded. No wonder the kind of tales and other folklore we have from that period does not reflect the range of what was available. In the presence of a missionary, who would, for example, tell a profane tale? Or, in the presence of a colonial official, who would sing an anti-colonial song or even admit that such songs existed?

It is sensible to note that the kind of tales we have reflect, at least in part, the kind of people that collected them. Cardinall notes that European collectors of tales had created certain expectations from the Africans such that "all Negroes know we expect the spider to be the hero."[24]

Folktales do not exist in isolation from other forms of folklore. They function in concert with songs, chants, riddles, jokes, and proverbs. Sometimes, for example, a tale elaborates on or exemplifies the truth of a proverb, whether the proverb itself is explicitly stated in the tale or not. There are tales which are told in the form of songs. There are tales which contain songs. While we think of riddles as short forms, we should also think of tales which are in fact riddles; the most typical forms of such tales are what scholars call dilemma tales, in which the audience is supposed to try and figure out a solution to the problem that the tale poses.

In teaching or studying folktales, it is important to think of this larger context and teach the tale as part of a network of folkloric discourses or at least to consider the ways in which each tale might relate to these other discourses.

As it is necessary to consider the tales as part of a folkloric system, it is also necessary to consider the tales and that whole system as a process. The tales interact in complex ways with these other forms, transforming and being transformed by them, illuminating and being illuminated by them, and dialoguing with them in many ways. It might make sense to describe this complex process as inter-orality.[25] These tales and the other folklore forms

---

[24] A. W. Cardinall, *Tales Told in Togoland* (London: Oxford University Press, 1931), p. 150.

[25] I suggested this term in my paper, "*Wimbo wa Miti*: An Example of Swahili Women's Poetry," *African Languages and Cultures*, 9, 1 (1996), p. 79.

interact with other social and cultural processes. Seen in this way, the folktale is a truly complex phenomenon, and the kind of study I have presented here is but a very small indication of this complexity.

Bibliography

Abrams, M.H. *A Glossary of Literary Terms, Sixth Edition*. Fort Worth: Harcourt Brace College Publishers, 1993.

Basehart, Harry W. "Cultivation Intensity, Settlement Patterns, and Homestead Forms Among the Matengo of Tanzania." *Ethnology*, XII, 1 (1973). 57-73.

_____. "Traditional History and Political Change Among the Matengo of Tanzania." *Africa: Journal of the International African Institute*, XLII, 2 (1972). 87-97.

Beidelman, T.O. *Moral Imagination in Kaguru Modes of Thought*. Bloomington: Indiana University Press, 1986.

Biebuyck, Daniel and Kahombo C. Mateene. *The Mwindo Epic*. Berkeley: University of California Press, 1969.

Cardinall, A.W. *Tales Told in Togoland*. London: Oxford University Press, 1931.

Dundes, Alan. *Cinderella: A Casebook*. Madison: University of Wisconsin Press, 1988.

Ebner, Elzear P. "Grammatik der kiMatengo-Sprache." 1957.

Gorky, Maxim. *On Literature*. Moscow: Foreign Languages Publishing House, 1935.

Häfliger, Fr. Johannes P. "Fabeln der Matengo (Deutsch-Ostafrika)." *Anthropos*, III (1908). 244-247.

_____. "Kimatengo Worterbuch." 1909.

Haring, Lee. "A Characteristic African Folktale Pattern," *African Folklore*. ed. Richard M. Dorson. Bloomington: Indiana University Press, 1979. 165-179.

International Center for Development-Oriented Research in Agriculture (ICRA). "Analysis of the coffee based farming systems in the Matengo Highlands, Mbinga District, Tanzania. Working Document Series 15." Wageningen: Agricultural University Press, 1991.

Kayuni, Yohani Chrisostomus Makita. *Habari za Zamani za Wamatengo.* Kipalapala: The Tanganyika Mission Press, n.d.

Lenin, V.I. "A Great Beginning." *The Lenin Anthology.* Selected and ed. Robert C. Tucker. New York: W.W. Norton & Company Inc., 1975. 477-488.

Mack, Maynard. Ed. *The Norton Anthology of World Masterpieces, Expanded Edition, Vol. 1.* Ed. Maynard Mack. New York: W.W. Norton, 1995.

Mbele, Joseph L. "*Wimbo wa Miti*: An Example of Swahili Women's Poetry." *African Languages and Cultures*, 9, 1 (1996). 71-82.

_____. Rev. of "The Sacred Buffalo People," a video on Native American culture and folklore. *Multicultural Education*, 2, 4 (1995). 36- 37.

_____. "How Hare Helped Civet." Translation of a Matengo Folktale. *Earthwatch* (July/August, 1993). 14-15.

_____. "Oral Literature and Social Protest." *Literature, Language and the Nation.* Eds. Emmanuel Ngara and Andrew Morrison. Harare: ATOLL and Baobab Books, 1989. 98-103.

_____. The Social Content and Function of Matengo Oral Literature. M.A. dissertation, University of Dar es Salaam, 1977.

_____. "Oral Literature Scholarship as an Arena of Ideological Struggle." Paper presented at the Second Annual Ibadan African Literature Conference, Ibadan, Nigeria, July 1977.

_____. "What Hare Did to Lion and Hyena." Translation of a Matengo Folktale. *Umma*, 6, 1 (1976). 80-82.

_____. "The Story of an Uncle and His Nephew." *Umma*, 5, 2 (1975). 92-96.

Ndunguru, Rev. Egino. *Historia, mila na desturi za Wamatengo*. Dar es Salaam: East African Literature Bureau, 1972.

Niane, D.T. *Sundiata, An Epic of Old Mali*. Trans. G.D. Pickett. London: Longman, 1990.

Petrie, William Matthew Flinders. *Egyptian Tales*. London: Methuen, 1895.

Pike, A. H. "Soil Conservation amongst the Matengo Tribe." *Tanganyika Notes and Records*, 6 (1938). 79-81.

Propp, Vladimir. *The Morphology of the Folktale*. Trans. Laurence Scott. Austin: University of Texas Press, 1968.

Rutatora, Deogratias F. "Strength and weaknesses of the indigenous farming system of the Matengo people of Tanzania." Indigenous Knowledge and Development Monitor, 5, 2 (1997). 6-9.

_____. et al. "Socio-economic issues revolving around indigenous knowledge systems and sustainable development in the Miombo woodlands of Mbinga district, Tanzania: a preliminary report." Morogoro: Faculty of Agriculture, Sokoine University of Agriculture. 1995.

Scheub, Harold. *The African Storyteller*. Dubuque, Iowa: Kendall/Hunt Publishing Company, 1990.

Schmied, D. *Subsistence cultivation, market production and agricultural development in Ruvuma region, southern Tanzania*. Bayreuth: University Press, 1989.

Seitel, Peter. *See So That We May See*. Bloomington: Indiana University Press, 1980.

Stenhouse, A.S. "Agriculture in the Matengo Highlands." *The East African Agricultural Journal*, 10 (1944). 22-24.

Sugimura, K. and D.F. Rutatora. "The socio-cultural and economic dynamics of the Matengo community in Mbinga district, Tanzania. A preliminary report of the Miombo Woodland Agro-Ecological Research Project." Faculty of Agriculture, Sokoine University of Agriculture, Morogoro, Tanzania, 1997.

Thompson, Stith. *The Folktale*. New York: Holt Rhinehart and Winston, 1946.

Willis, Roy. *There was a Certain Man: Spoken Art of the Fipa*. Oxford: At the Clarendon Press, 1978.

Yoneda, Nobuko. "On a Field Research of Matengo language." Proceedings of the First (and possibly last?) Meeting of the AFLANG, 1374 al Hijra.

_____. "The Impact of the diffusion of Kiswahili on ethnic languages in Tanzania: A case study of Samatengo." *Africa Urban Studies*, IV (1996).

Zimmer, Franz. "Die Wamatengo." *Mitteilungen der Anthropologischen Gesellschaft in Wien*, LX (1940). 304-323.